UNIX C SHELL DESK REFERENCE

Books from QED

Database

Managing IMS Databases
Building the Data Warehouse
Migrating to DB2
DB2: The Complete Guide to Implementation
and Use
DB2 Design Review Guidelines
DB2: Maximizing Performance of Online
Production Systems
Embedded SQL for DB2
SQL for DB2 and SQL/DS Application
Developers
How to Use ORACLE SQL*PLUS
ORACLE: Building High Performance Online
Systems
ORACLE Design Review Guidelines
Developing Client/Server Applications in an
Architected Environment

Systems Engineering

Software Configuration Management
On Time, Within Budget: Software Project
Management Practices and Techniques
Information Systems Architecture:
Development in the 90's
Quality Assurance for Information Systems
User-Interface Screen Design: Workstations,
PC's, Mainframes
Managing Software Projects
The Complete Guide to Software Testing
A Structured Approach to Systems Testing
Rapid Application Prototyping
The Software Factory
Data Architecture: The Information Paradigm
Software Engineering with Formal Metrics
Using CASE Tools for Practical Management

Management

Developing a Blueprint for Data, Applications,
and Technology: Enterprise Architecture
Planning
Introduction to Data Security and Controls
How to Automate Your Computer Center
Controlling the Future
The UNIX Industry
Mind Your Business

IBM Mainframe Series

From Mainframe to Workstations: Offloading
Application Development
VSE/SP and VSE/ESA: A Guide to
Performance Tuning
CICS: A Guide to Application Debugging
CICS Application and System Programming
CICS: A Guide To Performance Tuning
MVS COBOL II Power Programmer's Desk
Reference
VSE JCL and Subroutines for Application
Programmers
VSE COBOL II Power Programmer's Desk
Reference
Introduction to Cross System Product
CSP Version 3.3 Application Development
The MVS Primer
MVS/VSAM for the Application Programmer
TSO/E CLISTs: The Complete Tutorial and
Desk Reference
CICS: A How-To for COBOL Programmers
QMF: How to Use Query Management Facility
with DB2 and SQL/DS
DOS/VSE JCL: Mastering Job Control
Language
DOS/VSE: CICS Systems Programming
VSAM: Guide to Optimization and Design
MVS/JCL: Mastering Job Control Language
MVS/TSO: Mastering CLISTs
MVS/TSO: Mastering Native Mode and ISPF
REXX in the TSO Environment, 2nd Edition

Technical

Rdb/VMS: Developing the Data Warehouse
The Wonderful World of the AS/400:
Architecture and Applications
C Language for Programmers
Mainframe Development Using Microfocus
COBOL/2 Workbench
AS/400: A Practical Guide to Programming and
Operations
Bean's Index to OSF/Motif, Xt Intrinsics, and
Xlib Documentation for OSF/Motif
Application Programmers
VAX/VMS: Mastering DCL Commands and
Utilities
The PC Data Handbook
UNIX C Shell Desk Reference
Designing and Implementing Ethernet Networks
The Handbook for Microcomputer Technicians
Open Systems

QED books are available at special quantity discounts for educational uses, premiums, and sales promotions.
Special books, book excerpts, and instructive materials can be created to meet specific needs.

This is Only a Partial Listing. For Additional Information or a Free Catalog contact
QED Information Sciences, Inc. • P. O. Box 812070 • Wellesley, MA 02181-0013
Telephone: 800-343-4848 or 617-237-5656 or fax 617-235-0826

UNIX C SHELL DESK REFERENCE

Martin R. Arick, Ph.D.

QED Technical Publishing Group
Boston • Toronto • London

© 1992 QED Information Sciences, Inc.
P.O. Box 82-181
Wellesley, MA 02181

QED Technical Publishing Group is a division of QED Information Sciences, Inc.

Library of Congress Catalog Number: **91-26382**
International Standard Book Number: 0-89435-328-4

Printed in the United States of America
92 93 94 10 9 8 7 6 5 4 3

Library of Congress Cataloging-in-Publication Data

Arick, Martin.
   UNIX C shell desk reference / Martin Arick.
      p.   cm.
   Includes index.
   ISBN 0-89435-328-4
   1. Operating systems (Computers) 2. UNIX (Computer file) 3. UNIX
C Shell (Computer program) I. Title.
QA76.76.063A75   1991
005.4′3—dc20   91-26382
                                                        CIP

Table of Contents

Preface

Many users sign on to their UNIX system and then find themselves casting about for the correct command to use to get their job done. They have read those "manual pages" that are on the system that describe commands to run but still cannot seem to figure out what holds the whole thing together. The "glue" is right there under their fingertips, and the "glue factory" is overseeing every command and just waiting to be put to work to "glue" everything together. This glue factory is the "C shell." Most UNIX systems are set up so that when the user signs on, a C shell is triggered to provide a basic set of services, including interactive execution of commands.

If users understand what the C shell is able to do, they will become much more effective. In fact, the C shell provides a reasonably rich set of instructions and enough C–like facilities that the user can use it as a programming language. The user is able to put together small and large programs containing only C shell commands to help make repetitive tasks simpler. However, most users are ignorant of the power of the C shell, and use no more than a small portion of its facilities. They do not understand that the C shell remembers commands for recall and re-execution, and that the C shell allows the user to define a new set of commands that can be used either in addition to the usual set or instead of the commands that are already there. It is essential to understand that the C shell provides a programming language with control structures to allow sequences of commands to be defined, and a language to manage the flow through sequences of commands.

The first part of this book is designed to help the user apply the interactive features of the C shell more effectively, and to help the user develop another set of tailored commands. The second part addresses the more powerful command script language, and is heavily sprinkled with examples to demonstrate what works and what does not.

This book is organized by how the commands can be used and by what commands should be used together. No attempt has been made to exclude the use of the many other commands that most UNIX systems have, but the examples are designed to illustrate the most effective use of the C shell commands. One chapter of this book discusses the use of some of the other commands that exist on most UNIX systems but are not well understood by the average user.

This book and its examples have been developed on a particular implementation of the C shell. A number of these command scripts were attempted under two other C shells. Those that did not work have been eliminated.

A note is needed here on how to differentiate what appears *on* the terminal from commands that must be entered *at* the terminal for output to occur. The convention used in this book is that output on the terminal is underlined, text that needs to be inputted is shown in boldface, references to commands are shown in boldface, and references to files are shown in italics. Thus, <u>Enter login</u> is a string that appears on a terminal, **cd newdir** is a command entered on the terminal, and */usr/good/ .login* is the name of a file.

Finally, the author gratefully acknowledges the editorial help of Bess Arick, who has given unsparingly of her time to make this book much more understandable.

What Are the Capabilities of the C Shell?

OVERVIEW

A shell program insulates the user from the operating system by providing a set of functions that interact with the operating system. These functions include:

- managing the input from a terminal
- managing the output to a terminal
- defining new commands
- executing programs
- executing several programs at the same time
- remembering previous commands and re-executing them

This chapter will describe how the C shell provides each of these functions. To be able to execute the sample commands described in this book, the user must start a "user session" on the system; this chapter will also describe how to do that.

WHAT IS A SHELL PROGRAM?

A SHELL program is a program that isolates the user from direct dealings with the operating system. The SHELL program at your terminal is just waiting for you to tell it what to do. The SHELL indicates that by displaying a prompt (which can be any string of characters) and then unlocking the keyboard so you can type something in. You can request the execution of any of the UNIX commands that come with your UNIX system. In addition, the shell program will usually provide some functions that will help you manage input from a terminal and output to a terminal. Sometimes it is hard to separate the functions that the shell provides from the functions that the operating system provides. One of the advantages of the shell program is that it does not require you to know which functions are provided by what mechanism, so they can be mixed to provide the utmost capability.

HOW DOES THE C SHELL OPERATE?

The C shell executes in two modes. One is where it interacts with the terminal and executes commands entered from the keyboard—usually called "interactive". Another is where the shell executes a set of commands that are read from a file called a "command script". The lines in a command script are executed one at a time, as if they were separate commands entered from a terminal. A number of the commands the C shell provides operate differently when started from a terminal instead of from a command script, but the capability provided is much the same. In addition, there are some commands that operate only in a command script and some that work only in an interactive mode.

When the C shell is operating in an interactive mode, each command is entered from a terminal. While the command is being executed, the keyboard will be locked. If there is output from the command, it will then be displayed on the terminal. When the C shell is ready for another command, a prompt is displayed and the keyboard is unlocked.

It is possible to execute more than one command at a time by using the "background" function that the C shell provides. This will enable you to start a command and, while it runs, type other commands. The background command will continue to execute while being monitored by the C shell that started it. The C shell will notify you (if you wish) when any change in the mode of the background command occurs, as, for example, when it finishes.

THE C SHELL REMEMBERS

The C shell can remember all commands entered at the terminal. Such commands can be recalled and reexecuted or changed and reexecuted. In fact, pieces of previous commands can be reused and edited in later commands. All these "remembering" functions are called "history" functions. They form a basis for command line editing. All commands currently being remembered can be displayed so that the one you are interested in can be changed and reexecuted. A command can be reexecuted based on the name of the previous command, or its number in the history list. These history functions are further described in Chapter 3.

CONTROLLING THE INPUT AND OUTPUT FROM COMMANDS

Many commands produce output that can be saved or used as input for further processing. The C shell provides a number of methods for managing the output from commands, methods that let you save the output and use it as input for another command. Input from a terminal can be managed as well.

CREATING YOUR OWN COMMANDS

The C shell provides the ability to create your own command language, to define a new command, and to replace existing commands (even those the C shell provides) with commands of your own. For example, some commands have long names. You can, if you wish, define a one letter abbreviation of them. You can also change the default options of a command with options you prefer by redefining the command (and keeping the same name of the command if you wish). All these functions are accomplished with the "alias" function. The C shell searches its list of command aliases before it actually attempts to execute any command, whether the command is entered at the terminal or in a command script. Thus, any command, even the ones C shell provides, can be replaced.

DEFINING YOUR OWN VARIABLES

You can create, test, and manipulate your own variables to create commands or file names or even as input to commands. You can use them to specify conditions that can modify the flow through a command script. This capability is similar to the programming functions the C language provides.

The C shell defines some variables itself and, more importantly, examines some variables that control the way it operates. For example, you can decide what kind of prompt will appear on your terminal by defining a particular variable. You can decide whether to overwrite an existing file by defining or not defining a particular variable. All these variables are described in Chapter 7.

CREATING COMMAND SCRIPTS

If some sequences of commands are complicated but need to be used repeatedly, the C shell can execute a file of commands called "command scripts". These are created as is any text file, and can contain any UNIX commands or C shell commands.

In these scripts the order of the execution of the commands and conditions can be controlled and tested to determine their flow through the script. You can define your own variables and expressions to create the flow control you need. In fact, the C shell provides a special set of file attribute tests that can only be used in command scripts.

RUNNING MULTIPLE PROGRAMS
AT THE SAME TIME

The C shell can execute more than one program at a time. These programs can be "command scripts" or UNIX commands. All concurrently executing programs can be managed with a set of commands that halt execution, signal the programs, and determine their status.

STARTING A USER SESSION

When a user sits down at a terminal, the first thing usually seen is

```
login:
```

What the user must do at this point is enter his or her name. This will be echoed back and the following will appear

```
login: judy
judy's password:
```

Now the user enters a password. The password will not be echoed to the screen. The system will validate the user's name and password and, if all is proper, will start a terminal session. The moment the system recognizes the user's name and password, it starts a program to handle input from the user's terminal. This program is usually a shell program. Usually this program will be the C shell, but it is possible to choose any program to be run at the user's terminal. (Exactly how this is accomplished is discussed later.)

After the user's name and password are validated and accepted, the C shell has the user in its control. This is usually called "logging in". Two special files are read and executed in sequence when the user starts a terminal session, the *.login* and the *.cshrc* files. (How these files are used and what they contain is discussed in Chapter 15.) These two files will be executed and a "prompt" will appear at the terminal. The prompt indicates that it is the user's turn to enter a command and tell the C shell what to do. Every time the prompt is displayed, the user may type in a new command. When a prompt does not appear, it usually means the C shell is busy with some other operation and cannot accept a user's command at that time. Instructions on how to execute more than one command at a time are discussed in Chapter 10.

All information entered at the prompt is called the "command line". Normally, hitting the "return" key will terminate the command line and cause the C shell to process what has been entered. The first item that is entered (terminated by a blank) is assumed by the C shell to be the name of a command. Any items that are entered after the command itself are called "command line arguments," each of which is delineated by a blank. Arguments entered after a command that start with a hyphen ("-") are often called "command options" or "command modifiers". For example, entering

```
% ls -af
```

would request the execution of the command "**ls**" and would specify that the command line arguments are "-af". Only occasionally will UNIX command options not need the hyphen.

OTHER SHELL PROGRAMS

Several other shell programs are found on a range of UNIX operating system implementations. The most common, called the "Bourne" shell, is used to write scripts that the operating system uses. It lacks many of the interactive features the C shell has and thus is not as well suited for everyday use. Another shell, the "Korn" shell, has the command language for writing scripts and a set of interactive commands, but has not found its way into all UNIX implementations. This book concentrates on the C shell because it is found on a wide range of UNIX implementations and has both interactive and command script functions.

2

Managing Your Current Working Directory

OVERVIEW

To work with a file, it is necessary to know how to name it. This chapter will introduce the UNIX file system and the concepts of filenames, directories, and subdirectories. In addition, it introduces the relative naming of files and the idea of a "current working directory." The functions the UNIX shell provides for managing directories are discussed in this chapter and include

- **cd** command
- **chdir** command
- **dirs** command
- **popd** command
- **pushd** command
- **pwd** command

WHAT IS A DIRECTORY?

A typical UNIX computer system has many files, just as a business has many files. And just as a business has file drawers in a file cabinet, UNIX provides directories that organize files into groups. A business may also have several file cabinets to further organize groups of files, and UNIX allows directories to be hierarchically organized, too. Thus, directories can contain not only files, but other directories. A directory within another directory is called a "subdirectory." User files are usually organized by the person that owns them. System files are organized by their function. A typical UNIX file system looks something like this

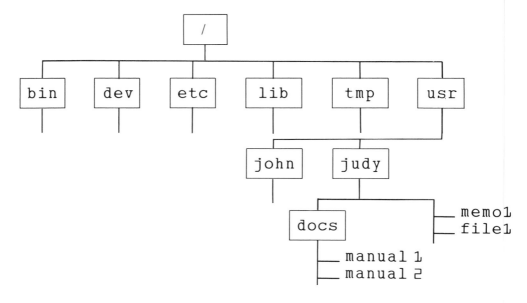

with each directory surrounded by a boxlike structure, and each file without one. In the picture above, *bin, dev, etc, lib, tmp,* and *usr* are all directory names. Within the *usr* directory are two more directories: *john* and *judy*. In this figure, only one directory, *judy*, contains both directories and files. The directory hierarchy can contain several more levels if so desired. The top level directory, "/" is usually called the "root" directory and contains both directories and files used by the operating system.

HOW ARE FILES NAMED?

Every file has a name that is referred to in commands. Each level in the directory structure is referred to by putting a "/" in front of the name of the level except for the root directory. The root directory is referred to by "/" alone. The *usr* directory would be referred to by */usr*. A file is referred to in the same way as a directory. Thus, the file *memo1* in the *judy* directory in the *usr* directory would have a full filename of

```
/usr/judy/memo1
```

and the file *manual1* in the lower level directory *docs* would have the full filename

```
/usr/judy/docs/manual1
```

Specifying the full name of a file every time you refer to it would be cumbersome, so UNIX allows "relative" file naming by assuming that any file name that does not start with a "/" is the name of a file relative to the directory currently being used. If you need to operate on files in the *judy* directory, instead of referring to them by preceding each name with */usr/judy*, UNIX allows operation in the */usr/judy* directory and reference to files simply by name. The simple rule of "relativity" is this: when the name of a file starts with a "/", that name must be the "full" pathname, and when it does not start with a "/", that name is relative to the directory the user is in. For example, referring to a file as "*memo1*" would indicate a file that is in the current directory, referring to a file as "*judy/memo1*" would indicate a file "*memo1*" that is in the subdirectory "*judy*", relative to the current directory. Referring to a file as "*/usr/judy/memo1*" would indicate a file in the */usr/judy* directory regardless of the current directory.

DISPLAYING YOUR CURRENT WORKING DIRECTORY

The current working directory is where the system will look for a file that is "relatively" named. The directory a user is in when first starting a session is usually set up by the system administrator. The first command many users learn is the one that shows the user what directory he or she is in. The **pwd** command accomplishes that. Thus, if you enter the command **pwd**, the system will display

```
% pwd
 /usr/fred

%
```

if your current working directory is *usr/fred*.

For example, if you wanted to copy one file to another, the system would look in the current working directory for the file to copy. If the file did not exist, you would receive the message "File not found." Actually, the **pwd** command is not a C shell command but one that reads a variable the C shell sets. It also contains the current working directory (see Chapter 7 on variables that have special meaning to the C shell).

CHANGING YOUR CURRENT WORKING DIRECTORY

The next important command tells the system to change the current working directory to a different directory. This command, **chdir** or **cd**, is followed by the name of the directory you want to use as the current working directory. If such a directory exists, the C shell will change the current working directory to the one that you requested. Thus, the command

```
cd /usr/lib
```

will change your working directory to */usr/lib*. The command

```
cd /usr/spool/lp/interface
```

will change your working directory to */usr/spool/lp/interface*. Any reference to a file or a directory that begins with "/" is a fully qualified filename or a "full pathname."

You can use a relative directory reference to indicate what directory you want to change to. Thus, if your current working directory is */usr/fred* and you enter the command

```
cd source
```

the system will try to change to the *source* directory relative to your current directory. Any time a directory is specified without a leading "/", the shell assumes it is a directory relative to your current working directory. Thus, **cd source** is equivalent to the command

```
cd /usr/fred/source
```

and both would set the current working directory to the same directory, */usr/fred/source*, if that directory exists.

You can also change to a directory that is in the same hierarchy as the current working directory but is not one of its subdirectories. For example, suppose that in the directory */usr/ fred* there are two subdirectories, *source* and *bin*. If your current working directory is */usr/fred/source*, how would you change to the directory */usr/fred/bin*? The command

```
cd /usr/fred/bin
```

would work, but a shorter command can specify the directory you want without specifying its absolute path. You can specify a relative directory path with the command

```
cd ../bin
```

which means move into the directory immediately above, and then down into the subdirectory *bin*. If you specify the command

```
cd ..
```

you will move up one level in the directory hierarchy. You can move up in the directory hierarchy as many levels as you like by adding more "../" specifications in the **cd** command. Thus, if you were in the directory */usr/fred/bin* and you wanted to move to the directory */usr/lib/macros*, you could use the command

```
cd ../../lib/macros
```

and move up two levels in the hierarchy, then down two levels to the directory of interest. The goal is always to use whatever information the shell knows to shorten the command you enter.

A user's home directory is special and can be returned to simply by entering the command **cd**. The home directory for another user is specified by a "˜" and is always so defined if that user has been defined on that system. If the "˜" is followed by a string of characters, the string of characters is assumed to be the name of a user and the home directory of that user will be substituted for the "˜" and the string. For example, the command

```
cd ˜harry
```

would change the working directory to the home directory of the user named "harry". This home directory is found in the password file and is assigned by the system administrator. The command

```
cd ˜harry/programs
```

would change the working directory to a subdirectory in the home directory of the user *harry*. Notice that with this notation, one need not know the home directory of the user *harry*.

MOVING TO A NEW DIRECTORY AND SAVING THE OLD ONE

The C shell will keep a list of directories you have been in if you use the command **pushd**. It will also remember what directory you are currently in as it switches you to the new directory you want. This command looks just like the **cd** command except that **pushd** replaces the **cd**. Suppose your current working directory is */usr/fred* and you want to move to */usr/fred/source*. You can use a relative directory name just as you did with the **cd** command and enter

```
% pushd source
 ˜/source ˜
%
```

If this new directory exists, your current working directory will be changed to */usr/fred/source* and the C shell will remind you that you used to be in */usr/fred*. Remember that "~" is your home directory. If you then enter

```
% pushd /etc
  /etc ~/source ~
%
```

and if that new directory exists, your working directory will be changed to */etc* and the C shell will remind you you used to be in */usr/fred/source* and *usr/fred*. So the directories you traverse in arriving at your current working directory are indicated. This can be thought of as a "stack" of directories. You "push" another directory on the "stack" of directories when you move to it with the **pushd** command. No matter how you specify the directory you want to change to, the stack of directories will always contain the full pathname of the current directory.

RETURNING TO A PREVIOUS CURRENT WORKING DIRECTORY

Now that you can save the names of the directories you have been in, you can use that information to return to a previous current working directory. To move to a prior directory, just enter the command **popd** and the current working directory will be changed to the previous directory on the stack of directories the C shell is maintaining for you. The name of the old current working directory is not saved. Entering the command **popd** will display

```
% popd
  ~/source    ~
%
```

and your current working directory will become */usr/fred/source*. Enter **popd** again and your current working directory will become */usr/fred*. Thus you can create a stack of directories with repeated **pushd** commands, and you can change to any of the entries on the stack with repeated **popd** commands.

DISPLAYING THE LIST OF PREVIOUS DIRECTORIES

There is also a command that displays what the stack of directories currently is. This command is for when you can't remember what directories you traversed to get to your current directory, and is called **dirs**. If you have used **pushd** as shown above, the output from **dirs** will be

```
% dirs
  /etc   ⁻/source ⁻

%
```

indicating that your previous directories were */usr/fred/source* and */usr/fred* (if your home directory is */usr/fred*) and that the current working directory is */etc*. You can display the full pathname for the directories in your directory stack by executing the command **dirs -1**. That would display

```
% dirs -1
/etc   /usr/fred/source   /usr/fred

%
```

if your home directory is */usr/fred*.

CHANGING TO ANY DIRECTORY
ON YOUR DIRECTORY STACK

You can move to any directory in your stack with the **pushd +n** command where **n** indicates what stack entry you want to change to. The stack of directories rotates preserving the order of entry. The first entry on the stack is number zero. The others are consecutively numbered, starting with number one. Look again at the previous output from the **dirs** command. If you wanted to change your directory to */usr/fred*, you would enter the command **pushd +2**. You would then see

```
% pushd +2
 ⁻ /etc   ⁻/source

%
```

indicating that the "+ 2-th" entry in the directory stack has been made the current working directory, and that the others have been rotated around the stack.

Executing the command **pushd +1** would change your current working directory to /etc and you would then see

```
% pushd +1
 /etc  /source
 
%
```

showing that the next entry has been moved to the top of the stack and that the others have been rotated. Three entries remain on the stack. Thus, the entries on the directory stack can be manipulated while moving to different directories, and all entries on the stack can be kept for later use.

Finally, **pushd** without any arguments will exchange the top two directories on the stack and preserve the contents of the stack while simply changing the order of the stack.

SELECTIVELY REMOVING ENTRIES
FROM THE DIRECTORY STACK

You can selectively remove entries from the directory stack by using the **popd** command with a relative number. The **popd +n** command will discard the n-th entry on the stack but does not change the current working directory. You can use this command to prune directory stack entries you no longer need.

For example, if the directory is stacked as in the last example, and you enter **popd +1**, you see

```
% popd +1
 /etc     
 
%
```

indicating the removal of one entry from the directory stack.

Of course, you can return to each of the other directories on the directory stack via the use of the **popd** command, but you lose that particular entry. Remember, **popd** (without any other arguments) will remove the top entry (the current working directory) from the directory stack. That entry can only be placed back on the stack by issuing the **pushd** command once again.

USING PUSHD AND POPD TOGETHER

One use of the **pushd** / **popd** pair of commands is to be able to move into a directory to perform an activity and then return to the directory you came from without ever knowing what directory you were in to start with. This pair of commands is particularly useful when constructing command scripts that need to be run in a particular directory. Using a **pushd** at the beginning of the command script and a **popd** at the end of the script will enable the script to start in one directory, to be in another directory while the script is running, and then to return to the original directory when it's finished. Users of your command script will not need to know that the command script operates in a different directory, and will not have to worry about what directory they are in when the script is done.

## 3

Using History Functions of the C Shell

OVERVIEW

The C shell can be instructed to remember all input that has been entered from the terminal, sometimes called "history." To illustrate the power of this, a user session that does not take advantage of this feature is discussed first. The same session is then reviewed while taking advantage of "remembering." The various features of the "history" functions are described later in this chapter.

The commands covered in this chapter include

- **history** command
- **set history** command
- **set histchar** command
- **source** command

A SAMPLE USER SESSION WITHOUT "HISTORY"

If you want to find a particular file and display it at your terminal, usually you would do an "**ls**" of the directory it is in. However, if you do not know which directory that is, what do you do? Suppose your directory structure looked like

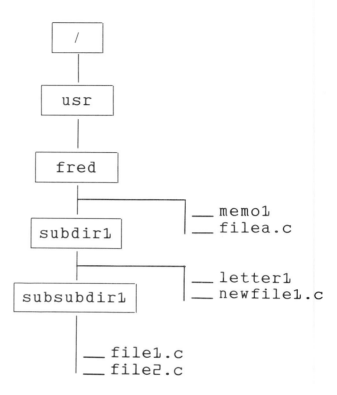

You would first execute an "**ls**" of your home directory, then look in each of the directories in that directory (subdirectories) until you find the file you are looking for. How many commands do you think that would take and how many keystrokes?

By doing an "**ls**" you get a list of files and subdirectories. Type "**ls subdir1**" to look in one of the subdirectories. You won't find the file there but you will find the subdirectory where the file will surely be. So you type in "**ls subdir1/subsubdir1**" but you are so excited you misspell the name of the subdirectory and type in "**ls subdir1/subsubdr1**" instead. You get back "file/ directory not found," so you retype the whole string again, "**ls subdir1/subsubdir1**" and this time you spell it correctly. You even have the correct directory, including the file you want to look at. So you finally type in "**more subdir1/subsubdr1/file1.c**" and get back "file/directory not found" because you spelled it wrong again. So you type "**more subdir1/subsubdir1/file1.c**" and, finally, you get the file you're after.

Let's review what you typed in (the numbers to the left have been added for clarity).

1. **ls**
2. **ls subdir1**
3. **ls subdir1/subsubdr1**
4. **ls subdir1/subsubdir1**
5. **more subdir1/subsubdr1/file1.c**
6. **more subdir1/subsubdir1/file1.c**

These six command lines total over 80 keystrokes. You could have saved a number of keystrokes if you had typed more accurately—or used the "history" function, in which case you would have typed in less than half the number of keystrokes.

A SAMPLE USER SESSION
USING "HISTORY" FUNCTIONS

If you could recall command lines you had already typed and either correct them for misspelling or add to them, the number of keystrokes could be lessened. The "history" functions the C shell provides are designed to do both those things, and many more, but first we will examine the simple operations. The history function is invoked by having one command line in your *.cshrc* file: **set history** = **100.** This tells the shell you want the last 100 command lines you entered to be remembered and recallable.

What difference would "history" have made in the example given earlier? The sequence that would have been typed would have been

1. **ls**
2. **ls subdir1**
3. **!!/subsubdr1**

    4. ˆdrˆdirˆ
    5. **more !$/file1.c**

Here, the numbers to the left represent the command number the history function uses to refer to each of these commands. In this example, we have used three basic "history" operations: "!!" means repeat the prior command and add whatever else is typed on the command line, "ˆ**drˆdir**ˆ" means replace "dr" with "dir" in the previous command and execute it, and "!$" means use the last field on the prior command line here. Thus, you would have typed in less than half the keystrokes and achieved the same result.

    To display the current history list with command numbers, issue the command **history**.

```
% history
   1. ls
   2. ls subdir1
   3. ls subdir1/subsubdr1
   4. ls subdir1/subsubdir1
   5. more subdir1/subsubdir1/file1.c
   6. history
%
```

Note the full command is recorded in the history file, not just the shorthand method for executing it.

PRINCIPLES OF "HISTORY" FUNCTIONS

The principle of using "history" is that each prior command line can be referred to by number (or context). Even each word in a prior command line can be referred to separately. Every command entered is numbered and stored in the history list so it can be referred to via its command number or a relative command number. In the prior example, command number three used a special operator ("!!") to refer to the prior command line and execute it. The operator "!2" would have referred to the same command because in the history list the command line #2 would have been the command of interest. Thus, "!n" refers to the command line numbered "**n**" and "**!-2**" points to the command line numbered two less than the current command number. If these entries are given by themselves, the command line is reexecuted. The command line can be added to before execution by typing, after the command line reference, any additional command line fields needed. In the example given for command #3, a reference to a previous command is given, and the additional field "**/subsubdr1**" was added to the rest of the previous command line to form a new command.

CONTEXTUAL REFERENCES TO PRIOR COMMANDS

History also provides a contextual way to refer to previous command lines. For example, "!ls" would refer to the most recently executed command line that began with "ls". In fact, "!l" would execute the exact same command line. In our example, both would refer to "!4". It is important to remember the user need not know what the number of the command line of interest is, only that the command you wish to perform started with "l" or "ls". If you have recently run two different command lines that each began with "l", you would have to specify the next letter(s) if you didn't want to execute the most recent command that began with "l". For example, suppose that the sequence of commands you had executed was (line numbers added for clarity):

```
22. more sample.c
23. more another.c
24. mv another.c another.sav
```

If the phrase "!m" is entered, you will execute #24. If you enter the phrase "!mo", you will execute #23. But suppose you wanted to rerun the last command that referred to the file "sample.c" but weren't sure what that command line was. Entering "!more s" executes #22.

Another method of contextual reference is provided by the "!?xxx?" phrase, which means execute the most recent command that contains "xxx" anywhere. Note that entering "!?sa?" would execute #24 and not #22. Entering "!?sam?" would execute #22. By the way, use of the "?..?" method to refer to a previous command from the past establishes the context for further command line references. Thus

    !?sam?:2 !$

refers to the second and last arguments on the most recent command line that contains "sam". Reference can also be made to the word that was matched by the context search with a "%".

REFERRING TO AN INDIVIDUAL WORD
IN A PRIOR COMMAND

Reference can be made to any individual word on any command line. Indeed, use can be made of any word on any command line and be combined with any other word on any other command line. The method for referring to an individual word is to refer to the command line containing that word using "!n" notation (or "!-x" notation), and adding a ":" operator and a number that is the relative position of the word of interest on the command line. In this context, 0 refers to the command itself, 1 is for the first argument on the command line, 2 is for the second argument on the command line, and so on. "!5:0" refers to the first word on the fifth command line, that is, the command "more". "!5:1" refers to the first word on the command line that doesn't include the command itself, in this case "subdir1/subsubdir1/file1.c". The special notation "!5$" refers to the last argument on the command line #5 which, in this case, is the same as "!5:1".

For example, suppose you need a copy of the file that was just found. You could type

```
cp subdir1/subsubdir1/file1.c \
            subdir1/subsubdir1/file1.c.bak
```

or you could use the history capability and type

```
cp !5$ !5$.bak
```

or, if you wanted to make the copy in the directory one above, you could type

```
cp !5$ !2:1/file1.c.bak
```

The goal is to type as little as possible and to use words that have been typed previously.

Now the "history" command would show

```
% history
   1. ls
   2. ls subdir1
   3. ls subdir1/subsubdr1
   4. ls subdir1/subsubdir1
   5. more subdir1/subsubdir1/file1.c
   6. history
   7. cp subdir1/subsubdir1/file1.c subdir1/subsubdir1/
   file1.c.bak
   8. cp subdir1/subsubdir1/file1.c subdir1/file1.c.bak
   9. history
%
```

Correction of the immediate preceding command line can be performed by using the "^" (usually called "hat") operand. For example, the command `^junk^goodstuff^` would replace *junk* with *goodstuff* in the prior command. This is a useful way of correcting misspellings in long command lines that have just been entered.

Reference can also be made to a range of words to be used. The command "**5:1-4**" (if there were that many words on the fifth command line) would refer to the first through fourth words after the command on command line #5. There are several special notations that refer to ranges of words. One special notation, "**!5***", refers to all arguments on the command line after the command. This is useful if it is necessary to change the command and keep the rest of the command line arguments. For example, before deleting a file, you can examine it using **more** or print it using **lp**. You can delete it using the command **rm !***. Another use of the "**!***" operand is to add some options to a command before reexecuting. For example, you use **grep** to search for a certain field in a file. Having found it, you want to know which lines the field is on. To search for the field, you would use the command

```
grep field to_search_for    file_to_search
```

To see the line numbers you need to add the "_1" option, but that may be difficult to edit into the command line. Another way is to use the command

```
grep -l !*
```

which adds the option "-1" to the previous command.

In addition, the special construct **!5:2*** indicates that the range of words to include is from the second to the last. Also, the !ˆ operand can refer to the first argument on the command line.

OPERATIONS YOU CAN PERFORM ON PRIOR COMMANDS

If you are not totally sure the command you remember is the right one to execute, you can preview it before executing it. Recalling the command line but not executing it can be accomplished by adding ":p" operator to the contextual reference. The command you referenced will be displayed but not executed. Thus, the command "**!5:p**" will operate as

```
%    !5:p
     more sample.c
%
```

This way you can modify the command before executing it. Obviously, you could modify it using ˆ or just reexecute it with the **!!** command.

One form of substitution operation was described earlier in this chapter. Suppose you want to make a different modification to the command line before executing it, but the modification is too complicated to use the "ˆ" operation. It is quite difficult to change " " (blanks) to some other field and, in addition, it is hard to add " " (blanks) in the middle of a command line. One operation for substitution uses the ":s" operator to modify strings in a command line. For example, examine command line #7 again, and suppose you want to change the file name from *file1.c* to *source1.c*. You would use the command

```
!!:s/file1/source1/
```

and the resultant command to execute would be

```
cp subdir1/subsubdir1/source1.c \
              subdir1/subsubdir1/file1.c.bak
```

which has had one substitution performed.

Suppose you need to change every occurrence of *file1.c* to *good1.c* in command line #7. That can be done with the "global" substitution operation. The command **!7:gs/file1.c/good1.c/** will change every occurrence of *file1.c* to *good1.c* whereas "**!7:s/file1.c/ good1/**" will change only the first occurrence of "file1.c" on command line #7. Changing every occurrence of *file1.c* would result in the command

```
cp subdir1/subsubdir1/good1.c \
              subdir1/subsubdir1/good1.c.bak
```

being executed. You can repeat a substitution that was just performed by using the ":&" operator as in the following sequence. Suppose you enter

```
cp /usr/fred/src/pgms/one.c \
              /usr/fred/src/pgms.bak/one.c
```

and that command fails because the name of the directory is not *pgms* but *bin*. If you enter the command **!!:s/pgms/bin/** to correct it, the command will fail again. You need only to perform the substitution again and the command will finally work. To do that you enter the command **!!:&** which performs the most recent substitution operation again.

One further substitution you can make uses a shorthand method (the "&" character) to specify a string. Substitution patterns are usually of the form **:s/old/new/**. However, if you just want to add some characters after the "old" string, you use the place holder "&" in the right hand substitution pattern. Thus, you would use the command **:s/old/&new/** to change the first occurrence of *old* to *oldnew*. You can make this a "global" substitution and replace every occurrence of *old* with *oldnew* by adding the "g" operand before the "s".

COMBINING HISTORY FUNCTIONS WITH OTHER SHELL COMMANDS

References to prior commands and any part of prior commands can be combined with any means of modifying the reference, such as the : operand. The command **!7:p** would simply redisplay the command as it was originally entered. On your terminal you would see

```
% !7:p
    cp subdir1/subsubdir1/file1.c
            subdir1/subsubdir1/file1.c.bak
%
```

which is the command you had entered.

If you want to turn your working directory into the one that contains the files you are copying, of course, you could enter

```
cd subdir1/subsubdir1
```

and your current working directory would become *subdir1/ subsubdir1*. However, there is a way to use the history functions to accomplish this. In the previous command you have a reference to the directory you want but that reference also contains the name of the file. But you need the directory without the filename to use the **cd** command with. To remove the filename specification and leave only the pathname, you would use the **:h** ("head") operand. That will strip off the filename and leave just the directory name. Thus, to change your working directory to the directory that contains the files that command #7 was operating in, you would enter

```
cd !7$:h
```

and your directory will change to *subdir1/subsubdir1*. There is a set of other modifications to file names described in Chapter 10.

DISPLAYING PRIOR COMMANDS ON HISTORY LIST

If you can not remember what commands are recorded in the history list, they can be displayed at any time by entering the command **history** by itself. After the example above, the command **history** would display

```
% history
   1. ls
   2. ls subdir1
   3. ls subdir1/subsubdr1
   4. ls subdir1/subsubdir1
   5. more subdir1/subsubdir1/file1.c
   6. history
%
```

The numbers displayed are the command line numbers and can be used to refer to a particular command line. Entering the command **!-2** would refer to command line #5, as would "!5". Notice that even though some of the command lines were created with shorthand phrases, the full command is stored in the history file. The history list is displayed with the oldest command first.

You can display the last n entries on the history list using the command: **history n**. If you do not specify a value after the command **history**, the entire history list will be displayed with the oldest command on the history list first. **history -r** will display the history list in reverse order with the most recent command first, and **history -r n** will list the last "n" entries in reverse order with the newest one first. For example, the command **history -r 3** would display

```
% history -r 3
   6. history
   5. more subdir1/subsubdir1/file1.c
```

```
    4. ls subdir1/subsubdir1
%
```

Finally, the command **history -h** will display the history list without any numbers. This is useful if you are creating a command script by executing the commands from your terminal one by one, and then capturing the sequence to a file for building a command script. This command can also be used to capture the current contents of the history list when you want to end your user session but reexecute it some other time.

SHELL VARIABLES THAT CONTROL HISTORY FUNCTIONS

As mentioned earlier, the size of the history list is defined by the variable history using a **set** command. A reasonable size— 100 to 200 entries—should be used. The history list does take up data space and a very large value may cause the C shell to use more memory in the computer.

You can change the "magic" characters that control command line substitution (default character is !) and quick substitution (default character is ˆ) by setting the variable histchar to the pair of characters you want to use.

The current history line number can be displayed in the prompt that is shown on the terminal by setting the *prompt* variable to contain the "%" character. Chapter 7 discusses setting the terminal prompt in more detail.

RESTORING A HISTORY LIST FROM A PREVIOUS USER SESSION

A history list that has been saved as commands can be restored at the start of a session with the **source** command. The command

```
source -h <filename>
```

will read in all the commands in the file *<filename>* as if they were entered from the terminal. It will not execute them though, and thus a history list is created. As indicated previously, the history list can be saved in a file without command numbers by redirecting the output from the **history -h** command in a file. So you can start up a terminal session with the same history list you ended the prior session with. Chapter 17 illustrates more fully how to save and restore your history lists.

ILLUSTRATING THE POWER OF THE "HISTORY" FUNCTIONS

One final sequence shows more of the power of "history." Say you want to edit a source file (after saving a copy of it) and then compile it. Often you must make a number of attempts to get the file correct. When you have finally gotten the file the way you want it, it is necessary to find out what the differences were between this file and the one you started with. You also want to print the modified file. This sequence would look like

```
cp !7:1 !7:1.bak
vi !6:1
```

(Substitute for "vi" the name of your favorite editor.)

```
cc !$
```

Now you repeat the sequence of editing the file and compiling it.

```
!vi
!cc
```

You can continue to alternately edit and compile the file without respecifying the name of the file. Just remember the numbers of the original command lines you used. When you have gotten the changes right and want to know what the difference between files was, type

```
diff !$ !$.bak > !$.out
print !$
```

Thus you can work with a file and specify its name only once.

One last note on using history functions. In most UNIX systems, there are operations you can accomplish only when you are operating as "root". However, it is difficult to remember for which commands you must be "root" to perform. Worse than that, most of the time those commands are fairly complicated and a chore to type. "History" provides an easy recovery mechanism because you can use the !! to repeat the previous command without typing it again. For example, you want to erase a file with a long filename like

```
rm /usr/sss/dirl/subdirl/work/source/filel.c
```

and the erase command fails because the file is owned by "root." You can reissue the command as

```
su root -c "!!"
```

which means "switch to the user 'root' " and issue the command that is in quotes. (If the 'root' user is password–protected, you will be asked for the password after you issue this command.) Thus, you have repeated the previous command while you are the right user for the command to succeed.

## 4

Handling Input and Output Interactively

OVERVIEW

Output generated by a command will be displayed at a terminal while input into a command will be expected to be entered from the terminal. This may not be convenient. It may be more useful to send the output from a command into a file, or get the input for a command from a file. This chapter describes how to redirect output into a file and redirect input from a file.

"STANDARD" INPUT AND OUTPUT
FILE DESCRIPTORS

When it is invoked, the C shell assigns three "standard" file descriptors. They are "standard input", "standard output", and "standard error". "Standard input" is the file descriptor that contains input for a command to process; "standard output" is the file descriptor to which output should be written; and "standard error" is the file descriptor to which diagnostic (error) messages should be written. Since these three file descriptors will always exist, most commands are written to use the contents of the files that the file descriptors name as you would expect: input is read from "standard input", output is written to "standard output", and error messages are written to "standard error". When the C shell is invoked from a terminal, all three descriptors are assigned to the terminal. Thus, when you invoke the command **more**, the output from that command will be written to "standard output", (the terminal), and input to that command will come from the terminal. As part of invoking **more**, a file can be specified and become the input source until the first page of output is displayed. Then input will shift back to the terminal.

REDIRECTING OUTPUT FROM A COMMAND

Commands often generate output. If the command is run at a terminal, the output will be directed to the terminal. In fact, users often run commands just for the output they produce. For example, the command **ls**, which will generate a list of files in a directory, will display that list at the terminal. If you run the command **ls -l**, you can get a list of files in a directory with each line of output describing a particular file and containing information on file size and the date of its creation. If a directory contains more than 24 files, the list will fill the terminal screen but not all files will be shown. Then the start of the list scrolls off the terminal, and part of the output becomes invisible. Worse, the list of files may be so long that the information you want may go off screen by the time you determine what file you are interested in.

There are a number of approaches to solving this problem. As discussed earlier, most UNIX commands follow the convention that output is written to "standard output" and that input is read from "standard input". Commands entered from a terminal have "standard input" and "standard output" assigned to the terminal. Further, diagnostic (error) messages are written to "standard error" and that is also written to the terminal. All possible approaches to "redirection" take advantage of the fact that output from a command can be redirected from the terminal to a file, or even be passed to another command.

To store the output from a command into a file, add the operator ">" to the end of the command line and follow with the name of the file you want to store the output in. Thus, the command

```
ls  > ls.out
```

causes the output from the **ls** command to be stored in the file *1s.out*. The operator ">" means redirect any output written to "standard output" into the file whose name appears to the right of that operator.

As another example, the command

```
ls -l  >  lslong.out
```

produces the longer list of files and the output would be placed in a file called *1slong.out*.

The redirection operator (">") will write the output into the file even if the file already exists. The contents of the file will also be deleted first if the file already exists. You can set a variable *noclobber* to stop this. With the variable set, if the file already exists, any attempt to write over current file contents will fail with the message: "<*filename*>: File exists". For example, the following sequence of commands

```
set noclobber
ls -l  >  lslong.out
```

will fail with an error if the file *1slong.out* already exists. You can overwrite the file under these circumstances by changing the ">" to ">!".

Suppose you want to build a file that is the result of output from a number of commands. The operator ">>" will append the output from the command into the file after the current contents. If the file does not exist, the file will be created—this is not considered an error. Thus, the sequence of commands

```
ls  -l  >>tmp/lslong.out
cd ../newdir
!ls
```

creates a file with output from the two different invocations of the **ls** command in two different directories. You need to use the full pathname for the output file because you will be changing directories to run another command. Unfortunately, this list would be hard to read because there will be an indication that one output set is from one directory and the second set is from another directory. That problem can be solved with

```
echo FILES from $cwd directory: >/tmp/lslong.out
ls -l > !$
cd ../newdir
!ec
!ls
```

which places the output from the individual **ls** commands into the file separated by a line that indicates from which directory these files come. Notice the use of "history" operands to save keystrokes. This set of commands also illustrates the use of the **echo** command that is built into the C shell. (Command **/bin/echo** will write out control characters, too.) The built-in **echo** command writes any words that follow it on the same command line to standard output so its output can be redirected to a file. Further, variable substitution is performed on the command line before the command is executed so variable *cwd* will be replaced by the current working directory when **echo** writes to standard output.

The redirection operator (">>") appends the output to the file if the file already exists, and creates the file if it doesn't. You can set a variable *noclobber* to ensure that the file exists. With the variable set, if the file does not already exist, any attempt to append to the file will fail with the message "<*filename*>: No such file or directory". For example, the following sequence

```
set noclobber
ls  -l  >>  lslong.out
```

would fail with an error if the file *lslong.out* did not exist. You can create a file under these circumstances by changing the ">>" to ">!". Then, whether the file exists or not, the file will be created if needs be, and the output will be appended to the end of the file.

REDIRECTING DIAGNOSTIC OUTPUT

If any errors are generated during the execution of a command, the error messages will be written to "standard error", not to "standard output". The operators ">" and ">>" will not redirect "standard error" so error messages will be written to the terminal. In order to redirect "standard error" and "standard output", the operator ">" must be changed to ">&" and the operator ">>" to ">>". Thus, the command line

```
command >& allmsgs.out
```

will ensure that any error messages generated by the command "command" are captured in an output file so they won't be lost. Unfortunately, the error messages will be mixed with the normal output you are trying to capture.

Separating the "standard output" from "standard error" is possible by building the following type of command

```
( command > std.out) >& std.err
```

This is really a two step redirection process. The first step takes place in a subshell operation and redirects standard output to a file *std.out*, while any error messages that are generated by this command are *not* redirected within the subshell. Outside the subshell, all output, including standard output and standard error, is directed to a different file. However, since the standard output has already been redirected to a file, the only output left to redirect will be standard error. Thus, one can redirect standard output to one file and standard error to another.

OUTPUT OF ONE COMMAND
AS INPUT TO ANOTHER COMMAND

Often the function required is to feed output from one command as input to a second command. When this type of operation is needed, the obvious solution is to have the first command write its output to a file and have the second read the file for input. As illustrated earlier, the execution of the command **ls -l** may produce a list that is too big to be shown on the terminal. Redirecting the output to a file, the user can examine the output one page at a time using the **more** command. Thus, the sequence of operations would be

```
ls -l  > lslong.out
more  <  lslong.out
rm  lslong.out
```

The awkwardness of this process is that a file has been created that is needed only briefly. It will soon have to be erased. It would be more efficient if some other agency manages the file creation and destruction process for the user. The C shell provides operators called "pipes". The creation of a pipe between processes can be invoked by inserting " | " between commands. This command sequence is called a "pipeline". Thus, to accomplish the task outlined above, issue

```
ls  -l | more
```

The pipeline operation connects the standard output of the command on the left side of the pipe to the standard input of the command on the right. If both commands follow the convention of standard input for normal input and standard output for normal output, this operation works. Thus, for the example given, after one page of output is shown on the terminal, the command **more** will pause, waiting for input from the keyboard before displaying another page of output on the terminal. Subsequent output is not lost but stored in the pipeline.

Since most commands take input from standard input and send their output to standard output, pipe commands enable the chaining together of a series of commands to accomplish whatever task is desired. One pipeline can be followed by a second or even a third. If a user wants to see the files in a subdirectory whose names end in ".c" sorted by size, the command line would be

```
ls -sl | grep '.c' | sort -r : | more
```

This will display file names sorted by size one page at a time.

It is also possible to activate a pipeline depending on the success or failure of a command with the operators " ‖ " and "**&&**". The pipeline set up by the operator " ‖ " will be executed if the execution of the command on the left side of the " ‖ " operator is successful, but will not be executed if the command fails. The pipeline set up by the operator "**&&**" will be executed if the command to the left of the "**&&**" operator fails, but not if that command succeeds. Try the following sequence of commands and note the expected output on the terminal.

```
% true :: echo this is true
  this is true
% false :: echo this is true
% true && echo this is false
% false && echo this is false
  this is false
%
```

The first command succeeds and a message prints. The second and third commands fail and no output occurs. Finally, the fourth command fails and thus a different message occurs.

Pipelining normally just redirects standard output. If you want to redirect standard error as well, change the ":" operator to the ":&" operator. As indicated earlier, the diagnostic messages will be intermixed with the normal output.

USING THE OUTPUT FROM ONE COMMAND IN ANOTHER COMMAND

The output from one command is often needed as input for another. Pipelining is one way of feeding the output of one command into another, but this only supplies standard output of one command as standard input to another. You may want the output of a command to be used as an optional argument to another command or as a command itself.

Command substitution causes a command to be executed as part of a more complicated command and to process the output from that command as substitution to be performed in the command. Command substitution can be caused by enclosing the command to be executed in ""'s (backward single quotes) within another command. The output from the execution of the command is broken into separate words at blanks, tabs and newlines. Then it's passed to the other command one item at a time. Often this type of substitution is combined with a **foreach** loop as in

```
foreach file ('ls dir1')
   .
   .
   .
end
```

This will process the list of files that the **ls** command provides. For a fuller discussion of the **foreach** command, See chapter 11. If you use ""'s instead, only the newlines force new words.

As another example, suppose you want to know the attributes of a command you have executed. You do not know the full pathname of the command, only that it's somewhere in one of your *path* directories. In most systems, the command **which** will find out of which directory the command is being executed. The following command

```
ls -l 'which which'
```

would cause the attributes of the command **which** to be displayed. This command line would operate in two steps. First the command **which which** would be executed to create the full pathname for the command **which.** When the command **which which** was finished, it would return the full pathname as the result. This result would be substituted for **'which which'** and the second command **ls -l** <**result**> would be executed.

SUBSHELLS AND SERIALIZING COMMANDS

Sometimes it is important to execute several commands before returning to the terminal for another command. Commands can be forced to run in sequence without interruption from the terminal by separating them with ";". Thus, the following set of commands

```
mv oldname newname; ls -l newname
```

is run without printing another prompt.

This would rename a file from *oldname* to *newname* and display the attributes of the new file before printing another prompt. The ";" operator lets you code more than one command on a line and separates one command from another to eliminate confusion over which operands belong to which commands.

This serialization of commands can be combined with the subshell operation to allow several commands to be executed in a subshell—that is to say, a new C shell—and then exit the subshell to perform other commands. Putting commands in a subshell is useful if you need to be in another directory to execute some commands and then return to the original directory to execute other commands. Thus

```
( cd; pwd) ; pwd
```

would change the working directory to the user's home directory, display the user's home directory, then return to the original directory and print that working directory. Note that the ";" operator separates the **cd** from the **pwd** command. In addition, any change to an environment variable that is made in a subshell will not be reflected in the parent shell.

REDIRECTING INPUT TO A COMMAND

Input to a command that has been started during a user session is expected to come from the terminal. Input to a command can also be redirected so it will be read from a file by using the operator "<". For example, the command

```
sort < inputfile > outputfile
```

will sort the records in the file *inputfile* and write the sorted records into the file *outputfile*. Of course, a command you execute in this way must be written to accept input from standard input and write output to standard output. Not all commands will so operate. Commands like **sort** or **more** do.

Input from the C shell itself can be redirected by using the operator "<<" and adding a "string" that will signal the end of the input. In this example

```
cat > file.out << EOF
happy
goofy
dreamy
sneezy
EOF
```

the input from the shell will be read into the command **cat** until the "string" (EOF) is read. Then the input to the command will be stopped. This example will cause a file (*file.out*) to be created. That file will contain four lines with the various names in it. (It will not contain "EOF".) This type of operation is useful if you want to build an input file to feed into a program, and want to do it in a command script. Substitution into any input line will occur before the command reads it in. Some commands read their instructions from "standard input" and thus can have the in-structions in the command script itself instead of in another file. For example, the stream editor **sed** can be set up to read from standard input the commands that it will run to edit a file. The end of this stream of commands will be signaled by "EOF" as above. Thus

```
sed file_to_edit << EOF
s/a/b/
w
q
EOF
```

would edit the file *file_to_edit* and change the first "a" on every line to a "b", write out this changed file, and quit.

To summarize, if you want to redirect the input to be from a file, use the "<" operator followed by the name of the file. If you want to redirect input so it comes from the terminal, use the "<<" operator followed by a string that will signal the end of the input from the terminal.

5

Defining Your Own Commands

OVERVIEW

If a particular command works better when certain options are specified, the definition of a new command or a replacement that specifies those options can be useful. The shell provides the ability to define your own commands by searching commands list you have defined (called "aliases") before execution. These definitions can be abbreviations for a particular command or the name for a set of commands you repeatedly use. In fact, even if a built-in command works unsatisfactorily, it can be replaced with a command that meets your needs and retains the same name.

The feature of defining or redefining commands is called "aliasing." The commands covered in this chapter are

- **alias** command
- **unalias** command

DEFINING YOUR OWN COMMANDS

Creating your own commands means defining them with the "**alias**" command. The C shell command **alias** is followed by the

name of the command you desire, and that is followed by what
the command should do in single quotes ("""). The following defines the alias *commandname*

```
alias commandname 'commands to execute'
```

so when you enter "**commandname**" at the prompt, what is
executed is 'commands to execute' even if "**commandname**"
matches a system command or is the name of a command the C
shell provides. This version of **commandname** is executed instead of the original **commandname** even if it is already defined. Thus, what replaces the built-in command called **cd** with
a more elaborate command is

```
alias cd 'cd \!*; echo $cwd'
```

The traditional **cd** command is thus replaced with a command
that not only changes to a new directory but also displays the
name of the new directory.

After a command is entered at the interactive prompt, the
C shell first checks to determine if an alias exists for it. The
aliased command will replace the command in the command line.
Any command line arguments that have been specified are added.
So any command can be replaced, even one provided by the C
shell such as **cd** or **pushd**, because the C shell will examine the
list of aliases before attempting to execute.

The commands used in the redefinition of built-in commands can contain the built-in commands themselves, as dem-
onstrated above. Standard C shell syntax is followed in the
replacement command, thus the reference to the built-in variable
cwd. However, a command's definition does not have to use the
built-in command it is replacing. It can use any command that
can be executed at the interactive prompt.

The aliased command can include history operations, too.
The history operation is applied to the unaliased command as
the most recent command on the history list. In the earlier example, that of a replacement for **cd**, the desired directory is
specified on the command line just as the built-in command
requires. The use of the "!*" in the definition of the alias is

standard for referring to all arguments on the previous command line after the command itself (as discussed in Chapter 3.) The "\" is needed to prevent the C shell from interpreting the "!*" before the final command has been created. If no reference is made to the arguments on the command line, they are added after the substitution for the aliased command is made. Thus, if you execute

```
cd  /usr/lib/macros
```

it would seem you really executed

```
cd  /usr/lib/macros
cd !*; echo $cwd
```

However, the only command that will show on the history list itself is the command **cd /usr/lib/macros**—even though the second command is what will be executed.

If the set of commands you want to execute is hard to describe on one line, you can define a command script to perform your commands and replace the built-in command with the execution of your command script, or to define a series of commands that, when combined, will function appropriately.

Alias commands can be stored in the *.login* file so when you start a new session you have a defined set ready. If you store alias commands in the *.cshrc* file, in addition to the interactive terminal session, every C shell command script you execute will have available to it the full set of aliases you have defined. Unfortunately, parsing a long list of aliases takes an extended period of time. A file of alias commands can also be set up. Those aliases could be defined for your interactive session with the **source** command. This will be discussed further in Chapter 8.

DISPLAYING THE ALIAS FOR A COMMAND

The complete set of **alias**es that are currently defined can be displayed by entering

```
alias
```

without any command line arguments. A list of all aliases and current definitions will be displayed. After starting a user session it is useful to be reminded of the **alias**es you have defined. The sample *.login* file illustrated in Chapter 17 displays the list of defined aliases on the terminal just before the first prompt is displayed.

To find out how a particular command has been aliased, enter

```
alias commandname
```

This will display how that particular command is defined. For example, if you had defined the **cd** command as described earlier and entered the command **alias cd,** you would see

```
% alias cd
  cd  cd \!*; echo $cwd
%
```

which is how it is currently defined. Notice that the ""''s that are part of the syntax of the alias command used to define this alias are not shown.

USING ALIASES AND SHELL VARIABLES WITHIN ALIASES

Aliased commands can be used within aliased commands. Suppose you want to have the prompt at your terminal indicate the current directory. Suppose you also want to display the contents of the new directory every time you change directories. The following aliases do that.

```
alias lf 'ls -aF'
alias cd 'cd !\*;lf; set prompt='$cwd"'
```

Any time you change directories, the contents of the new directory will be displayed and the prompt shown at your terminal will be changed to include the name of the current directory. Also, instead of coding the options of the **ls** command you wanted, a new command has been defined. That new command is then used in the alias for **cd**. Since every command is checked for an **alias** before execution, even coding an **alias** in the aliased command will work properly. The C shell sets a flag so it won't continue replacing a command it has already replaced.

To include the setting of the prompt and the listing of the directory contents every time you change directories, you will have to define aliases for **pushd** and **popd** as well as for **cd.** So to have a consistent set of aliases, the following should be defined.

```
alias  lf  'ls -aF'
alias  cd  'cd \!*;lf;set prompt="$cwd"'
alias  pushd  'pushd \!*;lf;set prompt="$cwd"'
alias  popd  'popd \!*;lf;set prompt="$cwd"'
alias  pu  'pushd \!*'
alias  po  'popd \!*'
```

Thus, any directory change operation produces an up-to-date prompt containing the current working directory. The last two aliases provide a shorthand notation for managing the directory stack.

Shell variables can also be used in an aliased command. (Chapter 6 describes how to define your own variables.) Any of those variables can be used in an **alias** command, too. If you want your terminal prompt to include the name of your current host, and you had defined a shorthand way of referring to the hostname with the **set** command

```
set hn='hostname'
```

You could change your **cd** and other like commands to include that definition as in

```
alias cd  'cd  \!*;lf;set prompt="$(hn):$cwd"'
```

That would mean any change in directory would cause not only the current directory to be shown at your terminal, but also the name of your current host.

REMOVING THE ALIAS OF A COMMAND

The current definition of an **alias** can be removed with the **unalias** command. The command **unalias cd** removes the redefinition of the **cd** command you entered earlier. Instead of using the exact name of the command you want to remove the alias from, you can specify a pattern to match. Thus, the command **unalias p*** would remove the alias of any command you had defined that began with "p". The command **unalias *** would remove all aliases you had defined.

ALIASING COMMANDS TO INCLUDE OTHER OPTIONS

Many UNIX commands have a variety of options that affect how they operate. One command used earlier, **ls**, has a myriad of options. Two that add a large amount of information without costing output space are the "a" and "F" options. If it is desirable to use those options every time you use the **ls** command, the following **alias** definition would do the job.

```
alias ls 'ls -aF'
```

With this definition, every time you enter **ls**, you execute the **ls -aF** command.

If you want to define an abbreviation for the **ls** command or a shorthand way of invoking the **ls** command, and you want the options to be used also, you can define another alias such as

```
alias l 'ls'
```

so that every time you enter the **l** command you execute **ls -aF**. The same idea applies to any command. You can define a whole list of one–letter and one–number commands for a shorthand way of invoking commands. Another favorite alias is

```
alias  m  'more'
```

because the **more** command is used so frequently to examine text files. On some systems the **more** command does not exist. Then you must provide an alias that references the **pg** command usually found on UNIX systems.

6

Defining Your Own Variables

OVERVIEW

Variables can be defined for use in the creation of your own commands. Two varieties of variables can be defined. One type is defined with the **set** command and is often called a "shell variable" because it is known only to the shell that defined it. A second type is defined with the **setenv** command and is called an "environment variable" because once defined it becomes part of the "environment" the shell is executing in and is known to any shell invoked later. This chapter will discuss the definition display, use, and deletion of both types.

The following commands are discussed in this chapter:

- *@*
- **echo**
- **printenv**
- **set**
- **setenv**
- **shift**
- **unset**
- **unsetenv**

USING SET COMMANDS TO DEFINE YOUR OWN VARIABLES

Variables can be defined and used within command scripts to create strings and integers whose values can be used and tested in command scripts. The syntax for the **set** command is

```
set var1 = stuff
```

which sets the variable *var1* to be the string 'stuff'. To create a variable for use as an integer, **set** the variable equal to an integer. The following command defines the variable *int1* to be an integer.

```
set int1 = 3
```

In a command script, or at the terminal, the value of that variable is used by putting a "$" before the name of the variable. Thus

```
cp $var1 savestuff
```

will copy whatever file is named by the variable *var1* (in this case, *stuff*) into the file *savestuff*. The value of the variable *var1* is substituted into the command by the C shell before it is executed. If the value of the variable *var1* has been made */u/fred/file1* by executing the command **set var1** = **/u/fred/file1,** then */u/fred/file1* is copied to *savestuff*. Variables can be defined based on other variables by referring to them in the **set** command itself. Thus, the command

```
set var2 = better$var1
```

makes the variable *var2* equal to "betterstuff" if the current value of the variable *var1* is "stuff".

Variables can be used anywhere in a command line, including in the command itself. For example, if the following two commands are executed

```
set rename = mv
$rename file1 file1.old
```

the file *file1* can be renamed *file1.old* if *file1* exists. To display the current definition of variables defined with the **set** command, issue the **set** command without any command line arguments. If the **set** commands outlined above—defining *var1, var2* and *rename*—have been executed, executing the command **set** without any command line argument will display the current values for those variables.

```
% set
  rename = 'mv'
  var1 = 'stuff'
  var2 = 'good stuff'

%
```

However, if you execute

```
set var3
```

the variable *var3* is set to null. One way to display the value of a particular variable is to pipe the output of the **set** command into **grep** and search for the variable of interest. For example, the following command will display the value of the variable *var1* (as well as any variable that contains the string "var1" in it).

```
set | grep var1
```

Using the **echo** command to do this is discussed later in this chapter.

DEFINING MULTIVALUED VARIABLES

An array of values can also be defined for a variable. This type of variable is called an "indexed" variable or a "multivalued variable" because each individual value in it is referred to by using a number as an index into the array. Each value in the array can be referred to and changed individually. The variable must be initially defined as an array of values by enclosing the set of entries desired within parentheses. Thus

```
set manyvalues = (first second third fourth)
```

will define the variable *manyvalues* to contain four values which are initially the strings "first," "second," "third," and "fourth." The number of values in the array associated with a variable cannot be changed without redefining that variable. Refer to the number of values in an indexed variable by placing a "#" between the "$" and the name of the variable. Thus

```
echo $#manyvalues
```

will display the value "4" at your terminal. Any individual entries in the values array can be changed by referring to the particular offset in the array using "[n]" notation. Thus, the following will **set** the second member of the array of values for the variable *manyvalues* to be 'notfirst':

```
set manyvalues[2] = notfirst
```

When the **set** command is used by itself to display defined shell variables, an indexed variable will show as a set of values enclosed by parentheses. A variable that is just a string of words will appear without parentheses. Try the following sequence of commands to illustrate the difference.

```
% set oneval = 'This is a string of words for fun'
% set mltvals = (This is a string of words for fun)
% echo "Variable oneval has $#oneval value(s)."
  Variable oneval has 1 value(s).
% echo "Variable mltvals has $#mltvals value(s)."
  Variable mltvals has 8 value(s).

%
```

The command **echo $oneval[3]** will fail with the message "Not that many elements", but **echo $mltvals[3]** will display "a".
    Elements can be added to an already indexed variable by

referring to the current values array, adding some values, and enclosing everything in parentheses. Thus

```
set a = ( first second )
```

followed by

```
set a = ( $a third fourth )
```

first defines a two—member array of values, then defines a four—member array for the variable a. Examining the value of the variable **a** using **echo**

```
% echo $a
  ( first second third fourth )
%
```

indicates the variable is an array of four values.

The C shell itself uses array variables for several of its special functions. The C shell sets up the *path* variable as an array of directories to search. Displaying the current value of the *path* at your terminal with

```
echo $path
```

will display a set of directories enclosed in parentheses. The shell stores this set of values of the variable so each can be used individually. In addition, each time a command is invoked, the shell sets up the variable *argv* to contain the name of the command and all its arguments.

The command **shift** can be used to move entries in an indexed variable to the left in the array, discarding the first entry on the list. For example

```
shift manyvalues
```

will move each entry in the variable *manyvalues* to the left, discarding the first entry. The following command sequence illustrates this.

```
% echo $manyvalues
  first notfirst third fourth
% shift manyvalues
% echo $manyvalues
  notfirst third fourth
%
```

It is an error if there are no entries in the variable to move or if the variable is not defined. The command **shift** without any arguments operates on the *argv* variable, discarding entries as it shifts entries to the left.

Variables defined by the **set** command are not passed to some other C shell that might be started. Thus, since running a command script will start a new C shell, any **set** commands executed in it will define variables local to that command script. When that command script is finished and that C shell terminates, those variables will no longer exist. In a certain sense, such variables can be considered private.

A variable can be changed at any time by executing another **set** command on that variable.

USING THE @ OPERATOR TO DEFINE A VARIABLE

The evaluation of an expression can define a variable. As discussed later, expressions can be evaluated with the "@" operator. This operator can be used to define a variable that contains the result of the execution of an expression. Thus

```
@ j = 10 * $a / 5
```

causes the variable *j* to be defined with the result of this calculation: "10 * $a / 5".

DISPLAYING THE CURRENT VALUE OF A SHELL VARIABLE

Since variables are referred to simply by putting a "$" before their names, displaying the current value of a variable is done by including the variable in an **echo** command. For example, if the variable *stuff* had the value "Hello world", then

```
% echo The variable stuff is equal $stuff
  The variable stuff is equal Hello world

%
```

would illustrate the variable's current value. The **echo** command can be followed by strings which are enclosed in "'' (single quotes), "" (double quotes), or nothing at all. Any variable following a "$" in a string enclosed in ""'s (double quotes) will be replaced by its value, but any variable following a "$" used in a string enclosed in "'' (single quotes) will not. In addition, the placement of a "\" before a "$" or any "$" followed by a blank, tab, or newline will prevent substitution.

For example, if the variable *stuff* had the value "Hello world", then

```
%   echo ''$stuff''
    Hello world

%   echo '$stuff'
    $stuff

%   echo ''\$stuff''
    $stuff
```

Entering the **set** command with no arguments displays all currently defined shell variables. This can be a fairly lengthy list because the C shell itself defines a number of variables (see Chapter 8 for details). As discussed earlier in this chapter, if you have defined a particular variable but do not remember its exact name, execute the **set** command and pipe its output into the **grep** command. Then look for the variable of interest. For example, if you think the variable you are interested in is called *username* or *userid*, but aren't sure,

```
set | grep user
```

will display any shell variables that contain the phrase "user" in their definitions or in their current value.

DELETING A SHELL VARIABLE

The value of a variable can be destroyed with the **unset** command. The command

```
unset stuff
```

will make the shell variable *stuff* undefined if it is **set** already. It is not an error for no variable to be **unset**. The word after **unset** may be a pattern containing any metacharacters like *, ?, etcetera. For example,

```
unset stuff*
```

removes the definition of any shell variable that begins with *stuff*. Incidentally,

```
set stuff
```

causes the value of the variable *stuff* to be the "null string", leaving the variable defined.

ENVIRONMENT VARIABLES

An "environment" variable can be defined as a variable that has all the properties of **set** defined variables with one addition: the definition of an environment variable is passed to any C shell that is started by the C shell in which it was defined. Because the variable becomes part of the environment executed by the new C shell, it is called an environment variable.

Environment variables are defined with the syntax

```
setenv WORK /usr/area/workarea
```

which defines the environment variable *WORK* as */usr/area/ workarea*. These variables and variables defined with the **set** command are referred to in the same way, by appending "$" to the name of the variable. They can be used in both command and variable substitution.

The names of environment variables are usually in upper case letters; **set** defined variables are in lowercase. This convention is convenient because when you examine a command script it is important to understand how to define a variable. Environment variables are often used so their definitions can be modified outside the command script itself. If no convention for naming variables is followed, users can't know how to modify their value without modifying the command script.

DISPLAYING THE VALUE OF AN ENVIRONMENT VARIABLE

The value of an environment variable can be displayed with a command some UNIX systems call **printenv**. For example

```
printenv WORK
```

displays (if the earlier **setenv** command was executed)

```
/usr/area/workarea
```

Issuing the command **printenv** without arguments displays all environment variables currently defined and their values.

Unfortunately, not all systems have the **printenv** command. Another way to display currently defined environment variables is to execute the **env** command. This displays all currently defined environment variables. To determine the current value of a particular variable with the **env** command, you pipe the output of the **env** command into **grep** and search for the variable of interest.

Environment variables are available to another C shell that is started by the C shell where the environment variable was defined. However, variables defined by **set** commands are not propagated to any subsequent C shell. Thus, if you run a command script executed under another invocation of the C shell, any variables you define via **set** commands will be unavailable during the execution of that command script. This difference between variables defined by **set** commands and those defined by **setenv** commands can be used to control the availability of definitions. To demonstrate this difference, enter

```
set  p = goodstuff
setenv  W  badstuff
```

These commands define two variables with the two methods. Now invoke another C shell with

```
csh
```

by itself. This starts a new C shell. Now, display the values of the two variables you just defined by entering

```
echo $p
echo $W
```

After the first command, you should receive the message "variable not defined". After the second you should see "badstuff". Thus, the value of the variable defined by **set** was not known and the variable defined by **setenv** was known. To terminate this invocation of the C shell, enter the **logout** command.

If the value of a shell variable is important to a subsequent C shell process, you can set the value of an environment variable from the value of the shell variable before invoking the new command script. For example, if the value of the shell variable *var1* is needed in the command, execute

```
setenv VAR1 $var1
```

This sets the value of the environment variable *VAR1* from the value of the shell variable and makes known to the subsequent C shell invocation the value of the shell variable *var1*.

DETERMINING WHETHER A VARIABLE IS DEFINED

To determine whether a variable is defined or not, test the expression **$?variable** for true or false. If it tests true, the variable is defined. If it tests false, it is not. (Chapter 12 gives more details on constructing and using tests.) Environment variables and **set** defined variables can be tested the same way. Namely, the expression

```
$?WORK
```

returns "true" if the variable *WORK* is defined and "false" if it is not defined.

In a command script, the command sequence is usually

```
if ( $?WORK ) then
      echo "WORK is defined to be $WORK"
else
      echo "WORK is not defined"
endif
```

to test whether the variable *WORK* is defined or not. This sequence will work correctly whether the variable is a shell or an environment variable.

It is not possible to determine whether a variable is an environment or a shell variable. You can test whether it is set or not, but not how it was set. If the practice is followed of using uppercase letters to define environment variables and lowercase letters to define shell variables, recognizing which type you are dealing with becomes obvious.

DELETING AN ENVIRONMENT VARIABLE

An environment variable can be destroyed by issuing the **unsetenv** command. Thus,

```
unsetenv WORK
```

causes the environment variable *WORK* to become undefined. The argument to the **unsetenv** command can be a pattern and contain any of the usual metacharacters like *, ?, etcetera, to select a set of environment variables to delete.

CONTROLLING SUBSTITUTING FOR VARIABLES

A variable is referred to by prefixing its name with a "$". Any characters after a "$" with no intervening space are considered part of the variable name. The end of a variable name is delimited with a "/", ".", "$", or a blank. For example

```
$jabc$kef.bak
```

would be substituted for by putting in the value for the variable *jabc*, the variable *kef* and adding ".bak" to create the final string. Sometimes, however, it is not possible to use one of the delimiting characters. For example, if a previously executed command was

```
set dirl=/usr/fred/src
```

and you want to display the contents of a file in the */usr/fred/ src1* directory, you might use

```
more $dirll/filel.c
```

but would fail with the message, "dir11 is not defined". It would be assumed that the name of the variable is *dir11* and not *dir1* as you wanted.

To solve this problem, the characters "{" and "}" can insulate the variable from the characters that follow the name of the variable you want to use when constructing variable substitution. Applying this technique you would use

```
more ${dirl}l/filel.c
```

to display the desired file. It is necessary to isolate the variable name from any following characters that might be interpreted as part of the name of the variable.

Substituting for variables can be controlled by the use of ""s versus "'s. Substitution for variables will always occur if "'s are used, but never if ""s are used. "$" can be printed by placing a "\" in front of "$". Substitution takes place after the command has been aliased.

## 7

Variables That Have Special Meaning to C Shell

OVERVIEW

Some features of the C shell can be controlled by the user. These features are managed by defining certain shell variables with **set** commands. There are also a number of shell and environment variables, whose value the C shell maintains, that the user can monitor to determine various aspects of the C shell operation. Each of these groups of variables is described in this chapter.

USER DEFINED SHELL VARIABLES WITH SPECIAL MEANING

There are a number of variables that can be defined by the user to control certain aspects of the user's interaction with the C shell. Many operate as a "toggle;" that is to say, they are either **set** or not **set**, either "on" or "off," and their value is not important. The sections that follow are organized alphabetically by variable name.

The *cdpath* shell variable defines a search path for subdirectories. This variable is described in Chapter 15.

The *histchars* shell variable can be defined to change the characters that are used to perform "history" operations. This variable is described in Chapter 3.

The *history* shell variable sets the size of the history file of previous commands, and is discussed in Chapter 3.

The *ignoreeof* shell variable is a toggle that controls the function of entering the [CTRL]+D characters at the terminal. If the variable *ignoreeof* is set, entering [CTRL]+D will be ignored by the C shell. However, if the variable *ignoreeof* is not set, entering [CTRL]+D causes the user session to end. Setting this variable will eliminate accidentally killing a session by mistyping. If the variable *ignoreeof* is set and *[CTRL]+D* is entered, the message "Enter 'logout' to end session" appears and the characters are ignored.

The *mail* shell variable contains directory name(s) that must be checked to determine if a new mail message has arrived for the user. The message "You have new mail." will appear at your terminal when a file in any listed directory has changed. Checking for new mail can be done after the completion of a command. If the first entry in the wordlist for the variable *mail* is numeric, then this is the number of seconds in the interval at which to check for mail. If the first entry is not numeric, the interval is set to ten minutes. For example,

```
set mail = (30 /usr/fred/Mail)
```

causes the directory */usr/fred/Mail* to be checked for new entries every thirty seconds.

The *noclobber* shell variable is a toggle that can prevent the unwitting overwriting of a file. When set, existing files cannot be overwritten using the ">" operand, and files that do not exist will not be created when using the ">>" operand. The operands ">!" and ">>!" can be used to suppress these checks against overwriting files.

The *noglob* shell variable is a toggle that can be set to stop the C shell from developing lists of filenames. "Globbing" is one operation that generates lists of filenames, and is discussed in Chapter 9. If a list of file-names has already been developed with "globbing", and it is not desirable for the C shell to provide further filename expansion, the *noglob* variable can be set. This is normally used in command scripts.

The *nonomatch* shell variable is a toggle that controls whether the failure of a "globbing" operation—an operation to find any filename that matches a particular pattern—causes an error that might halt the command script. If the variable *nonomatch* is not set, any globbing operation that does not find a filename to match the pattern causes the message "No match" to appear. In that case, the command script will fail. If the variable *nonomatch* is set, and if a "globbing" operation fails, no error message will be generated and the C shell command script will not exit, but will continue to execute commands.

The *notify* shell variable is a toggle that can be defined so every change in the status of an unfinished job is immediately reported. If the variable *notify* is not set, any change in the status of one of your jobs is presented only when a new prompt must be displayed.

The *path* shell variable defines a search path for executables. This variable is defined by listing directories to search for executable programs. When the execution of a program is requested and its name does not begin with a "/", the shell takes each entry in the *path* variable in the order specified, places it in front of the name of the executable, and attempts to locate it. If that operation fails, the next entry in the list is used the same way. If all attempts to locate the executable fail, the message "No such command" will appear. To provide a faster way to locate an executable, the contents of the directories listed in the *path* variable are "hashed" when the C shell reads the *.cshrc* file and every time the *path* variable is changed. If the contents of any directories change with the addition of new executables, it will be necessary to issue the **rehash** command. That will rebuild the "hash" table so the C shell can "locate" those newly installed executables. For the typical user, the usual *path* is

```
/usr/local  /usr/bin  /bin .
```

plus any of the local directories that contain widely used programs. For the user *root*, the usual *path* is

```
/etc /bin /usr/bin .
```

Normally the directory */etc* should not be in the *path* of a user because it contains only system commands.

The *prompt* shell variable defines the prompt that appears when the C shell is waiting for a command. This variable is set by the C shell if it is an interactive C shell and not a C shell command script. It can be changed into a string of characters and can include variables that will be substituted for before the terminal prompt is displayed. Even commands can be included. For example, the following definition of *prompt* will define the terminal prompt to be the current working directory.

```
set prompt="$cwd "
```

This command should be placed in the *.cshrc* file. Every time the prompt is displayed, the variable *cwd* will be substituted for. Often, the current command number is also of interest. To display the current command number, add "% (or !)" to the prompt. Thus, our example becomes

```
set prompt='$cwd % '
```

Finally, one other field users like to see is the host name. In heavily networked environments it is important to remind users of this. On many UNIX systems the command **hostname** does this. Thus, the above example would change to

```
set prompt="'hostname': $cwd % "
```

This will display the name of the host, the current working directory, and the current command number. Note that even in these shell variables command substitution can be used. The *prompt* shell variable is only definable in an interactive session. One way to detect an interactive session is to test whether the *prompt* variable is set or not. The following command tests whether the variable *prompt* is set. If it is, the command will set it to a user defined value.

```
if  ( $?prompt ) set prompt = "'hostname'; $cwd %"
```

The prompt will contain the host name, the current working directory and the current history command number.

Including the current working directory in your terminal prompt is very informative, but can cause a problem if the name of your current working directory is very long. For example, if the current working directory is "/usr/fred/goodprograms/scripts/bin/source/files", the prompt takes up half the typical command line of 80 characters—just to display the directory. Another approach is to show just the last two levels in the directory hierarchy. This can be done with the following definition of the *prompt* shell variable.

```
set cwd1 = $cwd:h
set cwd2 = $cwd1:t
set prompt = "'hostname': $cwd2 / $cwd:t %"
```

This definition takes advantage of the fact that variables are substituted for before processing. Of course, to show the current working directory, redefinition of the prompt variable in your aliases for the commands **cd, pushd, and popd** must be included. In the example *.cshrc* file, shown in Chapter 18, all these commands are aliased so that the prompt changes each time the current working directory changes.

The *time* shell variable can be defined so every command is automatically timed, and any command that exceeds a specified number of cpu seconds will cause a summary of resource usage to be displayed. More information on the use of *time* will be found in Chapter 16.

SHELL VARIABLES THAT ARE SET BY THE C SHELL

A number of variables are **set** by the C shell when it is invoked, and are also maintained by the C shell.

The *argv* shell variable contains the name of the command and the command line arguments arranged in an array of strings after a command has been invoked. The various strings in this array can be referred to either by number, or by the standard multivalue variable format. Thus, $0 (or *argv[0]*) contains the name of the command, $1 (or *argv[1]*) contains the first command line argument, $2 (or *argv[2]*) contains the second argument on the command line, and so on. *$#argv* contains the number of arguments in the array and is used to determine how many arguments were on the command line.

The *cwd* shell variable contains the name of the current working directory. Every time a **cd, pushd**, or **popd** command is executed, this variable is reset by the C shell to the name of the new current working directory. To set up a terminal prompt that contains the name of the current working directory, display the value of *cwd* in the prompt.

The *echo* shell variable is set by the C shell when the "-x" command line argument is used to invoke the C shell. When set, every executed command line is echoed to the terminal before it is executed. This variable can be set in a command script itself. This shell variable is further discussed in Chapter 8.

The *home* shell variable contains the name of the directory that is a user's home directory—where the user's files are stored. This directory is defined as part of the entry in the */etc/passwd* file that includes a user's name and password. The variable *home* helps provide an absolute pathname that is user oriented and individually defined. Thus

```
cp file1  $home/file1.bak
```

will be defined for every user and will copy a file from the current working directory to the user's home directory. Note that

```
cp file1 file1.bak
```

will also copy the file, but will create a back-up copy in the current working directory, and that directory may not be the directory of the user.

The *shell* shell variable contains the name of the file that the user is executing under. Thus, it is possible in a command script to determine if the expected executable is executing the command script.

The *status* shell variable contains the exit status from the last command and is maintained by the C shell itself. This variable can be tested to determine the success or failure of the previous command. When they fail, most commands cause the *status* shell variable to be set to a nonzero value. Built-in C shell commands that fail set the *status* variable to 1; those that succeed set it to 0. The exit status of a command script can be controlled with the built-in C shell **exit** command. That command will set the *status* variable to any desired value.

The *user* shell variable is set to the name of the user who has started the current user session either by logging in or by issuing the **su** ("switch user") command. This variable can be used to display the name of the current user by being included in the definition of the *prompt* shell variable. This variable can also be tested to ensure that the correct user is executing a particular command script. (Some C shells do not maintain this variable. You may have to use some other method to determine the name of the current user.)

The *verbose* shell variable is set when the "-v" command line argument is used to invoke the C shell. When set, every command is displayed on the terminal after history substitution and before execution. More discussion on this shell variable appears in Chapter 8.

The *$$* shell variable is set to the process number of the invoking shell. Any file name in a command script that needs to be unique can be defined with this variable. For example,

```
ls -l > /tmp/$$CC
```

will be expected to create a unique file name, even if it is the command script run over and over again in the execution of a command script. This variable can also be used if one must create a set of temporary files to be used in the command script, and also create unique, previously unused file names. In addition, this variable is unique because the process numbers are unique across the entire system. Thus, another user who might invoke at the same time, the same command will create a unique file since the *$$* variable will be set to a different number.

ENVIRONMENT VARIABLES THAT HAVE SPECIAL MEANING

A number of environment variables with special meaning are defined and maintained by the C shell when it is invoked. These environment variables are based on the value of certain shell variables the C shell defines and maintains. When any of these shell variables change, the respective environment variable changes also.

The HOME environment variable is the user's home directory and is the same as the *home* shell variable. The PATH environment variable is that set of directories to search for an executable, and is the same as the *path* shell variable. The USER environment variable is the login name of the user and is the same as the *user* shell variable. The values of these variables are available to any C shell command script because they are environment variables. The values of other shell variables defined with the **set** command are not.

8

Creating and Testing Command Scripts

OVERVIEW

Although many C Shell commands can be used interactively, a whole new world of personal command creation can also be exploited. Any commonly used command set can be made into a file that can be executed over and over. Such files are usually called "command scripts" and can be generalized so as to be made more useful. This chapter discusses the building of these command scripts. It discusses the following commands in particular

- **csh**
- **source**

GETTING STARTED WITH COMMAND SCRIPTS

A command script is created as is any text file, with a text editor. To create a command script, edit a file with the name you want the command script to have, add the commands you want to execute, and save it. Once you have saved this file you can execute it by entering its name. You must inform the operating system that this text file will be executed by marking it as executable. That is done by entering

```
chmod +x backitup
```

It is necessary to do this for any text file you plan to use as a command script.

To create a command script called *backitup*, edit the sequence of commands you want into a file named *backitup*. Mark this text file as executable. Execute it by entering the **backitup** command. The command script will be read from the disk and its commands executed one at a time, in the order they are in in the file. Chapter 11 illustrates how to control the sequence of commands if they are not to be executed in sequence.

Suppose there is an error in the execution of one of the statements in the command script. To fix it, edit the command script again and change the statement that is in error. Then save the changed command script and reexecute it. This process of editing and reexecuting the command script can be repeated as many times as necessary.

One necessary precaution is choosing a unique name for the file. Choosing a name that is used as a command somewhere else in the system will be confusing. What's more, the command script you wrote is the one you want to execute; it is not desirable to execute another script with the same name as yours.

Another precaution is ensuring that your file is marked as executable with the **chmod** command. Otherwise, UNIX will not execute your script and will give the message "Not an executable file".

Any valid command including the name of another command script can be used in a command script. Commands in a command script are executed in the order in which they are encountered except when C shell commands are executed, which changes the flow of the command script.

All C shell command scripts will begin by executing the *.cshrc* file. Thus, specification of the *path* variable in the *.cshrc* file will make the path available to all command scripts you execute.

ENSURING THAT THE CORRECT SHELL EXECUTES YOUR COMMAND SCRIPT

There is another shell on most Unix systems, the "Bourne" shell, which will usually execute your command script if you do not specify otherwise. Every command is passed to the Bourne shell first for execution. So you must tell the Bourne shell you want the C shell to execute this command instead. It is necessary to choose one of the following methods to indicate that the C shell is to execute your script. There are at least three ways to do that.

With some versions of UNIX, if you start your script with a line that begins with a "#" (comment), the Bourne shell will pass the execution of your command script to the C shell. Unfortunately, this is not always recognized, and should be avoided.

A second way, more universally accepted, is to indicate the shell you want by having the first line of the script indicate it. The syntax is

```
#! /bin/csh
```

if you want to use the C shell. Note that if you want your script executed by the Bourne shell, you only have to change "csh" to "sh" in the line shown above. Anyone wanting to execute this command script will know under which shell to run it. In addition to specifying the shell under which to execute, options can be added to the invocation of your script by simply coding them on the same line with the full path and name of the C shell. The following command causes both the "f" and "v" options to be invoked when a command script is executed:

```
#! /bin/csh -fv
```

How these options work is explained in detail later in this chapter. The important idea here is that these options (and others) can be specified on the same line that indicates under what shell to execute.

A third way to ensure that the C shell executes your script is to invoke the C shell directly and enter as an argument the name of the command script you want to execute. Thus

```
csh backitup
```

executes the command script *backitup* under the C shell. In addition, when you invoke the C shell directly in this fashion, you can specify, on the command line, under which options you want the script to run. Thus, to run your command script with the **f** and **v** options, you would enter

```
csh -fv backitup
```

to run the command script *backitup*.

CREATING A SCRIPT FROM COMMANDS ENTERED AT A TERMINAL

Some sequences of commands are often used repeatedly. You may not be aware of these sequences until you have used them. Since all your commands have been saved in the history list, you can use that facility to help you create a command. In fact, one approach to creating a command script is to execute the commands one by one at the terminal to make sure the sequence will do what you want.

After you have entered the commands at the terminal, enter

```
history -h 20 > mycommand
```

This captures the last twenty commands entered into the *mycommand* file. The "-h" option removes the number from the list of commands saved. Now edit the *mycommand* file and remove the commands that are not needed or correct the ones that are in error. The next time you want to execute the same sequence of commands, they will be saved and ready.

COMMENTS AND CONTINUATION LINES IN COMMAND SCRIPTS

Comments can start anywhere on a line. They begin with "#" and end with "newline". Thus, the following are both valid comments for a command script

```
cp stuff stuff.bak  # Make a backup copy
# If this operation is successful, we will delete
```

It is good practice to start a command script with a set of comments that describe what operation the script performs, what the command line options (if any) are, and what the input and output files are. A description like this is handy, since the next time this command is used, what it does and how to use it will be readily available.

Each command script line is expected to be a different command. However, it is possible that a particular line may be excessively long or just difficult to read. A one line command can be broken up into multiple lines with continuation characters ("\") at the end of every line that is a continuation of previous lines. Thus, the following is equivalent to the example above.

```
# Make a backup copy
cp \
stuff \
stuff.bak  # This is another comment.
```

No character can follow the "\" character. Of course, using too many continuation lines causes command scripts to be difficult to read and understand. Continuation lines are useful when it is necessary to break up a line longer than 80 characters. The C shell can execute a line with over 80 characters, but on a terminal that line will be hard to work with. For scripts to be continually useful, they will probably be modified and changed a number of times, and must be readable so changing them is easy.

PASSING ARGUMENTS TO THE COMMAND SCRIPT

Suppose you want to create a command script that makes a backup copy of a file and, furthermore, you want it to be general enough to allow the creation of a backup version of any file by just naming the file when you invoke the command script. The command

```
backitup bestpgm.c
```

would create a copy of the file *bestpgm.c*.
The command

```
backitup bettrpgm.c
```

would create a copy of the file *bettrpgm.c*. Thus, when you invoke the **backitup** command, you add to the command line the name of the file you want to backup.

The internal variable *argv* is defined every time you invoke a command script. This variable is an array of pointers to the various command line arguments. The entries in this array are referred to as *argv[0], argv[1], argv[2],* and so on. Further, this variable contains the number of arguments that were on the command line and can be tested to determine that number. For example, create this command script and save it as *parrot*.

```
#! /bin/csh -f
# This command script will echo back the arguments
# on the command line using the argv array notation.
#
echo "There are $#argv arguments on the command line."
echo " The command = $argv[0]."
if ($#argv > 0 ) then
echo " The first argument on the \ command line = $argv[1]."
endif
If ($#argv > 1) then
echo " The second argument on the \ command line = $argv[2]."
endif
```

The use of *$argv[0]* is just a way of referring to the first element in an array which, in this case, is the command itself. By extension, *$argv[1]* refers to the second element in the array, which is the first argument passed to the command. Now attempt the command **parrot stuff and nonsense**, and you should see

```
% parrot stuff and nonsense
There are 3 arguments on the command line.
The command = parrot.
The first argument on the command line = stuff.
The second argument on the command line = and.

%
```

Incidentally, note that to determine the number of arguments in *argv*, you refer to it in the usual way—by specifying the number of values as *$#argv*. The "$" in front tells the C shell that this is a variable that was previously defined and that the "#" refers to the number of values in this array variable. Note also that the contents of each value in a variable can be tested for. Multivalued variables are covered in more detail in Chapter 6.

A shorthand way to refer to the command line arguments is to use "$0" as the command itself, "$1" as the first argument on the command line, "$2" as the second argument on the command line, etcetera. Take the *parrot* script and edit it to look like this:

```
#! /bin/csh -f
# This command script will echo back the arguments
# on the command line using the $0, $1, type of
# variables.
#
echo "There are $#argv arguments on the command line."
echo "The command = $0."
if ($#argv > 0 ) then
  echo" The first argument on the \ command line = $1."
endif
If ($#argv > 1 ) then
  echo'' The second argument on the \ command line = $2.''
endif
```

```
If ($#argv > 2 ) then echo" The third argument on the \
command line = $3."
endif
```

Now when you enter the command **parrot stuff and nonsense**, the following output should appear.

```
% parrot stuff and nonsense
There are 3 arguments on the command line.
The command = parrot.
The first argument on the command line = stuff.
The second argument on the command line = and.
The third argument on the command line = nonsense.

%
```

To illustrate another point, edit the *parrot* script once more and change all the "'s (double quotes) to 's (single quotes). The script will now look like

```
#! /bin/csh −f
# This command script will echo back the arguments
# on the command line.
#
echo 'There are $#argv arguments on the command line.'
echo ' The command = $0.'
if ($#argv > 0 ) then
  echo ' The first argument on the \ command line = $1.'
endif
If ($#argv > 1 ) then
  echo ' The second argument on the \ command line = $2.'
endif
If ($#argv > 2 ) then
  echo '' The third argument on the \ command line = $3.''
endif
```

This time all the double quotes have been replaced with single quotes to show how these different string operators are managed. Now execute the command **parrot stuff and nonsense** again.

You should get

```
% parrot stuff and nonsense
There are 3 arguments on the command line.
The command = $0.
The first argument on the command line = $1.
The second argument on the command line = $2.
The third argument on the command line = $3.

%
```

The point of this exercise is that the single quotes prevent substitution. Hence, the variables do not get replaced in the output.

DEBUGGING COMMAND SCRIPTS

The C shell provides several facilities to help you test your command script, and there are several ways to invoke these facilities. Some can be specified only by command line arguments, either when invoking the script, as in

```
csh -<options> commandname
```

or on the line in the script that specifies under which shell to execute, as in

```
#! /bin/csh -<options>
```

In some cases, a shell variable that will enable the facility can be defined. The following describes each of the command line arguments available and whether they can be invoked via internal options.

To test the syntax of your shell script, you can execute it with the "-n" argument on the csh command you use to invoke the command script, or code it on the line in your script that specifies that you want the C shell to execute.

This option will cause the shell to parse each command in the script to test that the command lines are correctly specified. Any syntax error will be reported, but no other checking and no other processing will be performed.

To display every command line before it is executed and before any substitution has occurred, specify the "-x" option on the command line, or define the *echo* shell variable in the beginning of your command script. Either method causes each command to be echoed to standard output as it is being executed. Any error messages or output that occurs during the execution of the command script will be displayed right after the command line that caused it.

If you want to display every command line after history substitution has been performed but before execution, specify the "-v" option on the command line, or define the *verbose* shell variable. As with the "-x" option, each command will be echoed to standard output but this will occur after substitution. Thus, this option combined with the "-x" option causes command lines to be displayed before and after substitution and substitution's intermixing with output as commands are executed. Examining the command line after history substitution lets you see if the command you expected to be executed is in fact being executed. You can also see how the condition testing in your script is being handled.

To cause the C shell to terminate the command script when any command terminates abnormally or returns a non-zero exit status, specify "-e" on the command line. This option is useful if the status of each command is not being individually tested during the course of the script, and if you want the failure of an individual command to halt the script.

To start a command script faster, specify the "-f" option on the command line or on the command script line that specifies under which shell to execute. This option will cause the C shell not to read the *.cshrc* file upon start up. This saves time because the reading and processing of a lengthy *.cshrc* file takes time. Most of the contents of the *.cshrc* file are not useful in a command script. Because shell variables are not available to a subsidiary shell, no *path* variable is defined and no **set** variables from the *.cshrc* file are known to the subsidiary C shell. However, environment variables will be known to this subsidiary shell and thus the PATH variable will be known.

The echo and verbose options can take effect even before the execution of the *.cshrc* file by specifying the "-X" and "-V" options, respectively, when invoking the C shell. Enabling these options that early provides a way to debug your *.cshrc* file. When you start a new C shell, the *.cshrc* file is executed before any commands in the command script, thus any command in the *.cshrc* file will be echoed to the terminal before it is executed. Any error in processing the *.cshrc* file will be shown just after the command has been executed.

Commands can be fed into a C shell from standard input by using the "-s" option. Also, an interactive C shell can be started with the "-i" option. C shells are always interactive if their standard inputs and outputs are assigned to terminals. A new interactive C shell can be started by entering the **csh** command. By entering the **exit** command, you can leave it.

To execute just one or two commands under a separate shell, specify the "-c" option when you invoke the C shell. If the commands fail, you will not be disturbed because the failure will occur in a subshell. For example,

```
csh -c 'source file1; command1'
```

will cause just the two commands between the single quotes to be executed under a separate C shell. The C shell will then exit and return to the parent shell.

Another case where the "-c" option is necessary is when a command script is invoked from a program using a "system" call. In this case, the only operation required from the C shell is to execute a command script under the C shell. However, when "system" calls are executed, the Bourne shell gets to execute it first, and the Bourne shell needs to be told the C shell is to execute. Thus, in a program this would look like

```
system ("/bin/csh -fc 'command_to_execute'");
```

and the command **command_to_execute** would be run. Even if that command fails, the program that invoked it would continue.

If you specify the "-t" option, one line of input is read and executed.

SERIALIZING COMMANDS

Normally, individual commands are placed on separate lines. Several commands can go on the same line if they are separated by ";". In that case they are executed serially. Command sequences of this sort can be executed as components of pipelines by enclosing them in parentheses. These commands are then executed in a subshell that maintains its own set of shell variables. This construct is most often used when some commands must be executed in one directory and the rest of the script in another.

Commands can be executed without waiting for their termination by following them with an "&". This is called "backgrounding a command" and is discussed in detail in Chapter 11.

Conditional pipelines can be formed using " ‖ " and "&&". This sort of pipeline allows different commands to be executed depending on the success or failure of the first command. Thus

```
command1 || command2
```

means that if the execution of **command1** is a success, **command2** will not be executed. If the first command fails, the second command will be executed. Conversely

```
command1 && command2
```

means that if the execution of **command1** is a success, **command2** will be executed, but not if the execution of **command1** is a failure. As an example of the use of conditional pipelining, try

```
false && echo this will only appear \ if the command is true
```

Nothing will appear on the terminal. Do it again but replace the **false** command with **true**. The output of the **echo** command will appear. Each of the above commands can be replaced with a set of commands by enclosing them in parentheses, as discussed earlier.

The most powerful command construct is the use of "'s to

cause a command to be executed, and for the results of that execution to be substituted into the command line that contains it, one result at a time. This construct is discussed further in Chapter 14.

EXECUTING A FILE OF COMMANDS IN THE SAME C SHELL

If it is necessary to execute a series of commands in the same C shell you want to keep in a separate file, you use the **source** command to execute them. Normally, if you execute a set of commands that are in another file, another C shell will be invoked—a subsidiary process. In that case, any changes to the environment (new shell variables, even environment variables) that occur in that invocation will not be seen by the parent C shell process. If you want those changes to be reflected in the parent's process environment, use the **source** command. That command executes commands from a file under the same C shell. Then any changes to the environment will be seen by the current C shell.

To use the **source** command, create a file that has the commands that change the environment in it (usually **setenv** commands and **set** commands). Now execute

```
source <filename>
```

to cause these environment variables to be defined in this C shell.

GOOD PROGRAMMING PRACTICES FOR C SHELL SCRIPTS

A number of programming practices exist for writing command scripts and they should be followed to make your scripts more useful and maintainable.

The first line of a command script should contain the name of the shell under which it is to run. This will ensure that the correct shell executes it, and will also indicate what kind of command language is used. The next section should contain comments that describe what the script does, what the command syntax is, and what the various arguments to this command should be. It is also useful to include discussions of what files are used for input and output.

The first section of executable code should test each of the expected command line arguments and verify that they are what they should be. If two arguments on the command line are expected, your command script should validate that two arguments were specified. If fewer arguments than you expect are specified, display messages that inform the user what the correct syntax for the command is and what the various arguments mean. For example, if you have a script called *copyme* that will copy the contents of one file to another, and it is expected that both filenames be specified on the command line, have the following statements in your script:

```
#
# This script will copy one file to another.
#
# The first argument on the command line will be the
# input file and the second argument on the command
# line will be the output file.
#
if (#$argv < 2) then
  echo "Not enough arguments on command line."
  echo "Expected syntax is:"
  echo "  copyit inputfile outputfile"
  echo " "
  echo "  where:"
  echo "  inputfile is name of file to copy"
  echo "  outputfile is name of file to copy into"
  exit (1)
endif
  ~
  ~ (rest of command)
  ~
```

Remember, the user of your command may not know exactly what the syntax for the command is, so your command should be prepared to say so. Executing it without arguments results in a message that will instruct in constructing the correct command line. The **exit (1)** command shown in the command script will cause the execution of the command script to halt at that statement. The *status* shell variable will be set to "1" to signal the failure of this command. Thus, an error in command line arguments will produce a message like

```
% copyme file1
Not enough arguments on command line.
Expected syntax is:
    copyit inputfile outputfile

    where:
    inputfile is name of file to copy
    outputfile is name of file to copy into

%
```

This way, if an error occurs that is related to the initial command line arguments, the user will be able to determine what was incorrectly specified.

When they fail, command scripts must give the user enough information about the problem or about what error occurred in processing. The C shell itself does not give much information when a command fails, other than some message akin to "No such file". No indication is given as to which file is not found. All possible conditions should be tested for and messages that indicate what the error was should be displayed.

You should manage the *status* your command script will show when it is done executing. It is good practice to set the *status* shell variable to a nonzero value when the command script fails. Conversely, if the command succeeds, you should ensure that the value of the *status* variable will be zero by using the **exit** command to set the exit status to zero.

One final good programming practice is to either fully qualify the names of the commands you need to use, or to manipulate the *path* shell variable to contain the directories storing commands you refer to in the command script. If you modify the *path* variable, set it back to the original value when you exit the command script. The following example illustrates how to save the current value of the *path* shell variable, modify its value, and reset it when you are done.

```
# Save current path for later
set oldpath = $path
# Change current path to have the added
# file directories you need
set path = ( /etc /usr/bin $path )
 .
 . (execute your commands here)
 .
# Now reset your path variable before exiting
set path = ( $oldpath )
```

Thus the command script provides a method for the C shell to find the commands that the script will execute.

9

Creating and Modifying Lists of Filenames

OVERVIEW

In order to perform operations on all the filenames of a particular type in a directory, a list of those filenames is needed. For example, it may be desirable to compile all the files in a directory that end in ".c". This chapter discusses how to develop a list of filenames that contains just those names you want it to, and a number of operations available to determine each component of the name of the file once you have found the file that interests you. Using the individual components it will be possible to create the name of a new file and to check any components of the name of the file. Finally, this chapter discusses how to create a uniquely named file.

DEVELOPING LISTS OF FILENAMES USING METACHARACTERS

Certain characters such as *, ?, [ ], or { } are used to form patterns to match filenames against. These characters are called "metacharacters" because they perform certain operations in which they are more than just characters. A pattern is created using these metacharacters and any other characters. All filenames that fit the pattern are placed in an alphabetical list. Earlier this operation was called "globbing". It is considered an error if a "glob" operation does not find any matching filenames. If no patterns match, the message "No match" appears. If this error occurs in a command script, the command will exit with the message. If the *nonomatch* shell variable is **set,** the failure to find a filename that fits that pattern is tolerated and the command script continues.

In some places in a command script it may be important to stop the globbing operation. This is done by **set**ting the *noglob* shell variable.

CREATING FILENAME PATTERNS

The metacharacter "*" in a pattern will match any string of characters including the null strings. Thus

```
ls source*.c
```

will return any names that start with *source* and end with *.c*, including names like *source.c, source123412.c*, and even *source ___.c*. The pattern string *s*c* will produce a match for all of these names too, but also will have matched *silly.c* or *sxxxxxxxxxxxxxxc*—which may not be what you want. The command **ls *.c** will find any file ending in *.c* while the command **ls *.*** will match all files in the current working directory. The list of filenames is alphabetically sorted before it is returned.

The metacharacter "?" can be used when any one character in a pattern is to be matched against. A null match cannot occur. Thus, the command **ls source?.c** will match files with names like *source1.c, source2.c*, but will not match files with names like *source12.c* or *source.c*. If it is desirable to match two characters in a file name, code two "?"s. Thus, the command **ls source??.c** will match *source11.c* and *sourceab.c* but not *source.c* or *source1.c* or *source123.c*.

The metacharacters "[" and "]" are used to define a closed set of characters that can be matched between two particular strings. Thus, the pattern *x[abc]z* will match filenames such as *xaz, xbz,* or *xcz* but no others. The characters between "[" and "]" define a closed set of possible matching characters. A range of characters to match against can be coded using a "–". Thus, the pattern *x[a–g]z* will match the previous filenames but will also match *xdz, xez,* and even *xgz.*

The metacharacters "{" and "}" are used together to specify names to be created from substitution strings that are listed between the { and the } in the pattern. So

```
a{g, h, i}p
```

will expand to the filenames *agp, ahp,* and *aip,* but to no other filenames. This is really a shorthand type of notation and not a globbing operation at all. To further illustrate this, try this **echo** command.

```
% echo {1,2,3}{a,b,c}
  1a 1b 1c 2a 2b 2c 3a 3b 3c
%
```

The following **ls** command is one way to list the attributes of several files at once.

```
%  ls  -l  /dev/tty{0,1,2,3,4}
  crw-rw-rw  1  bin mra 4 , 0 /dev/tty0
  crw-rw-rw  1  bin mra 4 , 1 /dev/tty2
%
```

This shows the attributes of some terminal devices. This list type of pattern matching can be combined with any other metacharacters such as "*". Thus

```
ls -l /dev/tty{0,1,2,*3,4}
```

will match files named */dev/tty0, /dev/tty1, /dev/ttyg3, /dev/tty3, /dev/ttyp3,* and even */dev/tty4.* The order of file names matched is preserved within the "{" and "}" operands, but the file names that match the "*3" operand are sorted in order. Thus, this list of files that match will not be sorted in alphabetical order but the order of the list will be preserved.

If any pattern match starts with "/", it must be matched exactly. Thus

```
ls -l /abc/def*.c
```

matches the file */abc/defnn.c* but not */ghi/abc/def1.c* or even */abc/ghi/defnn.c*.

The metacharacter "˜" at the beginning of a filename is a reference to a user's home directory. When the ˜ is followed by a user name, the shell searches for that name in the */etc/passwd* file and substitutes the home directory of that user. Thus

```
ls -l ˜ken
```

will change to

```
ls -l /usr/ken
```

if */usr/ken* was the home directory of the user *ken*.

MODIFYING FILENAMES

Filenames can be modified to get only the parts of their full name you need. Each such operation uses the ":" operand with a letter that indicates what operation is to be performed. Usually these operations are applied to filenames that have been obtained by either a history operation, a command substitution operation, or an expression to develop filenames. They make it possible to break a filename into its components and rebuild it into another name.

One simple operation is the removal of the extension part of the filename. To do this, modify the filename with the **:r** ("root") operand. If the full filename is */usr/fred/source/program1.c*, applying the ":r" operand to it results in the filename */usr/fred/source/program1*. Another simple operation is to get the extension alone. That is done with the **:e** ("extension") operand. To illustrate further how these two operands work, try the following series of commands.

```
foreach file ('ls')
echo "The file is called: $file"
echo "The file without extension is called: $file:r"
echo "The extension is called: $file:e"
end
```

This set of commands will display, one at a time, each of the file names in your current working directory and, following the name, the name of the file without the extension, and the extension itself. (The use of the **foreach** command is discussed in Chapter 11.)

Another operation is the removal of the trailing filename altogether. In this case you end up with the directory name all by itself. This operation is accomplished with the **:h** ("head") operand. Thus, if you have entered

```
ls -l /etc/inittab
```

and you now want to change your working directory to that directory, you can do so with

```
cd  !$:h
```

which changes your current working directory to */etc*. This example also illustrates the use of these operands in modifying the parts of a prior command that is recalled using history operations. For further discussion of history operations, see Chapter 4.

Another useful operation is removing the pathname and leaving only the filename available. This is accomplished with the **:t** ("tail") operand. If you enter

```
ls -l /usr/fred/source/program1.c
```

you can isolate the name of the file with the **:t** operand as in

```
cp  !$:t  !$:t.x
```

This command makes a copy of the file *program1.c* as a file named *program1.c.x*. Only one of these ":" operands can be used at a time, so if two operations are needed on the same filename you will have to create intermediate variables. To illustrate this, enter

```
ls -l /usr/fred/source/program1.c
set pathname = !$:h
set nopathname = ! -2$:t
set noextname = $nopathname:r
```

Now enter the following **echo** commands to display the current value of the two variables.

```
% echo "No path name is: $nopathname"
No path name is: program1.c

% echo "No extension name is: $noextname"
No extension name is: program1

%
```

This lets you make a copy of the file without including the ".c" extension. The command

```
cp $pathname/$nopathname $pathname/$noextname.x
```

will make the copy with the name you want.

If you want to make a copy of all files in a directory that end in ".c", the resulting file should not be named *filename.c.bak*. The filename should be *filename.bak*—without the ".c" in the middle. You can do this by stripping the extension from the filename. Try the following script to make a copy of all the files in the */usr/fred/source* directory that end in ".c".

```
#
# Make a copy of files that end in ".c"
# as filename.x
#
foreach file ('ls /usr/fred/source')
if ( $file:e == "c") then
  cp $file $file:r.x
endif
end
```

All copies will be filenames whose names end in ".x" and do not contain ".c".

A substitution can be applied to a filename coming from a history operation with the **:s** ("substitute") operand. For example, if a set of files had been named *program1.c, program2.c*, etcetera, and you want to change the names to *good1.c, good2.c*, etcetera, you would enter

```
ls  -l source1.*
mv  !$ !$:s/source/good/
ls  -l source2.c
mv  !$  !$:s/source/good/
```

This will list the attributes of the files in category *source*.c* and rename them by building a new name that consists of the old name with its "source" part replaced with "good". This kind of operation only works in history–based operations.

If you want to change all instances of a string in a command, add the "g" ("global") option to the substitution operand. The global substitution operation works only on the first instance of the string in each word of the command. Each filename will be considered just one word. For example, to copy a file from one directory to another, enter

```
cp /usr/fred/source/file1.c /usr/fred/dest/file1.c
```

To copy *file2.c*, enter

```
!!:gs/1/2/
```

which will cause the command

```
cp /usr/fred/source/file2.c /usr/fred/dest/file2.c
```

to be executed. Then you can copy *file3.c* by applying the same kind of operation.

Any previous command in your history file can be printed by adding the ":p" ("print") operand to the reference you use for the command of interest. Thus

```
!!:p
```

will display the previous command without executing it, and

```
!23:p
```

will display the command numbered 23 in the history file without executing it.

If you have a multivalued variable that contains filenames or directories and you apply the ":h" operation to it, only the first entry in the variable will be changed. To change all entries in a multivalued variable, use a ":gh" operand instead. Thus, if the *path* shell variable was defined as

```
/usr/fred/bin /etc /usr/local /usr/bin
```

try the following **echo** command:

```
% echo $path:gh
/usr/fred /usr /usr

%
```

This command is the result of applying the ":h" operation to each value of the *path* shell variable. Note that the result of applying ":h" to the filename *etc* is null.

If you have a multivalued variable that contains filenames or directories and you apply the ":t" operation to it, only the first entry in the variable will be changed. To change all entries in a multivalued variable, use a ":gt" operand instead. Try the following sequence of commands to understand the effect of the ":gt" operand.

```
% echo $path
/usr/fred/bin /etc /usr/local /usr/bin

% echo $path:gt
bin  etc  local  bin

%
```

This is the result of applying the ":t" operation to each value of the *path* variable.

CREATING A UNIQUE FILENAME

Sometimes it is necessary to create intermediate files that will be processed by another command. These files will store data to be added to another file, or to be processed and replaced in another file. Commands like **sed** process data files as input. "Standard input" is where the commands to control **sed** are read. In all such cases it is desirable to create a file for data storage. The file name should be unique not only to the user, but also within the user's directory. That can be done with the *$$* shell variable, which is the process number of that instance of the C shell. Each invocation of the C shell has a unique process number, so the variable *$$* will be unique. Thus, the filename

```
/tmp/$$CC
```

will be unique for each invocation of the C shell and can be combined with other methods of naming files.

## 10

Running Multiple Commands at the Same Time

OVERVIEW

Commands are often entered one at a time, and their completion is something you wait for. However, it is possible to start several commands at the same time (or in some sequence) and not wait for any of them to end before entering more. Commands that are started but not waited for are usually called "background" commands or "background jobs." Commands that are waited for are called "foreground" commands or "foreground jobs." Since a command script is only a set of commands, the term "job" will be used to mean commands by themselves or command scripts. "Jobs" are all managed the same, whether they contain just one command to execute or a long, complicated script. Only one foreground command can be executed at a time while an almost unlimited number of background commands, within *some* operating limit, can be executed. This chapter discusses how to start background commands, how to check their status, and how to control them.

In addition, this chapter covers the following commands:

- **bg**
- **fg**

- **jobs**
- **kill**
- **nice**
- **onintr**
- **stop**

CREATING BACKGROUND COMMANDS

Any command can be placed in the background by adding a "&" at the end of the command line. The "&" has other meanings when found in the middle of the command line. When a command is entered with the end of the command line containing a "&", the C shell will display

[1] 346

which indicates that this is background job #1 with process id number 346.

The output the background command generates will be displayed just as if it was running in the foreground. Generating output to your terminal in a background command does not stop its execution. Since you can execute another command with one already running in the background, any output that may be created by this other command will be interspersed with the output created by the background job. Managing that will be discussed later in this chapter.

On the other hand, if the background job is set up to request some input, it will halt until that input is sent. When it needs input, the background job will simply wait and not resume execution until that input is received. You can start a job in the foreground and then place it in the background by interrupting its execution with *[CTRL]+Z* at the keyboard. The command will halt, the message "Stopped" will appear on your terminal, and the prompt will be displayed. You can then put the job in the background by issuing the **bg** command. The execution of the job resumes in background mode and another prompt will be issued asking for another command. If the job is left suspended, no further execution will occur—but the job won't quit, either.

Thus, you can start a command in the foreground, wait to see that it is working correctly, and put it in the background. Or you can start a command, wait to see its first output, and suspend execution while you run some other command. After you have finished the other command, you can resume execution of the suspended job.

DISPLAYING THE STATUS OF YOUR JOBS

The command **jobs** will display the status of each job you have started in the background that is still running. The output from the **jobs** command looks like

```
% jobs
  [1] - Stopped    <command>
  [2] + Stopped (tty output) <command>
  [3]   Running    <command>
  [4]   Stopped (tty input) <command>

%
```

This indicates that there are four jobs with three in various states of "stopped" and one actually running. The "+" by one of the jobs indicates it was the job most recently started or most recently signaled. The "−" indicates the next most recent job.

The C shell is informed whenever a process changes state. It will tell you (on the terminal) of any change in status of any job you are running if the *notify* shell variable is **set**. In fact, you can execute some other command, for example, even editing a file, and the message from the shell will be displayed in the middle of whatever output is on the terminal at the time. In the case of normal completion of the job, this message looks something like

```
[1] Done <command>
```

which indicates that job number 1 has finished executing normally. If the *notify* shell variable is not **set**, the shell will notify you only when it displays a new prompt. The command **jobs −1** lists the status of your jobs and the process id numbers of each. The process id of your jobs can be quite important, as we shall discuss later.

If a job exits with a non-zero exit code, that code will appear in the message provided it indicates the background job is finished. This message will look something like

```
[2] Exit - 48 <command>
```

which indicates job #2 ended its execution with a status of -48. Another way to display what the jobs are doing is to use a non–C shell command **ps** (process status). On most systems, if the command **ps -p** <**process id**> is entered, the terminal displays what command being executed that is associated with the assigned process id. This is the same process id displayed when the job starts, or is shown in the **jobs −1** command output.

CHANGING THE MODE OF A JOB

Any suspended job or any job currently in the background can also be made to run in the foreground by entering the **fg** command. This command restarts the execution of the suspended job, but in the foreground, so no prompt appears. If there are several jobs in various states of execution, you must enter the job number after the **fg** command to indicate which job you want to run in the foreground. The output of the **jobs** command shown above indicates the job number. The command

```
fg %3
```

brings the third job into the foreground, where the "%" stands for "job number." If a job is suspended and must be executed in background mode, enter the command %1 **&** to put job number 1 into the background and resume its execution. In addition, reference can be made to a job with a string that is the start of the command being executed. The command %**ls** would refer to a job that is running a command starting with the string "ls" and bring that command from background to foreground execution. Further, the job displayed with a " + ", as indicated by the **jobs** command, can be referred to by "% + ", and the job with a " − " can be referred to as "% − ".

SIGNALING YOUR JOBS

Jobs you have started in the foreground can be cancelled by entering the [CTRL] + C characters. As indicated earlier, entering the [CTRL] + Z characters will suspend a foreground job.

Jobs that have been started and are running in the background can be signalled with the **kill** and **stop** commands. You can usually halt the execution of a job by issuing the **stop** command. For example, if you issue

```
stop %2
```

you halt the execution of job #2. This causes its status to change to "Stopped (signaled)" as shown by the **jobs** command. To restart your job, you issue **bg %number** to restart it as a background job, or **fg %number** to restart it as a foreground job. Some commands will not respond to these signals.

The **kill** command can send a number of signals to a job or process that has been started. (You need extra privileges to signal a process you did not start.) If the job is equipped to handle that signal, its mode can be changed. There are a number of signals, both numeric and phrase-like, that can be sent to a job. These signals can be displayed by entering the command **kill −1**. Although a discussion of signals is beyond the scope of this book, in general the **kill** command is used to destroy a job. If you issue the **kill %2** command, you will usually cause job number 2 to end its execution. The message

```
[2] Terminated  <command>
```

will appear on your terminal. You can issue **kill -STOP <process id>** to suspend a job's continuing execution. You use the "<process id>" for signalling a job you did not start. The job can be restarted by issuing the **kill -CONT <process id>** command. Occasionally jobs will not respond to most signals and you may need to use the **kill −9 %2** command to end their execution without any recovery.

There is no default **kill** signal, so simply entering **kill** at the terminal without any reference to a job will not send a signal to the current job. The **kill** command can be combined with the **onintr** command, discussed in the next section of this chapter, to provide a way to signal commands running in the background.

MAKING COMMAND SCRIPTS NON-INTERRUPTIBLE

Commands can be executed so they can not be interrupted with the **onintr** shell variable. This command can take several forms. The first is simply

```
onintr
```

which restores the original handling of interrupts by the shell. Usually the shell terminates scripts on an interrupt when they run in the background, or will return to the terminal input line when they run in the foreground.

The second form that causes all interrupts to be ignored is

```
onintr -
```

which means this script can be suspended only by entering [CTRL]+Z characters when the command is running in the foreground. This command will not respond to [CTRL]+C characters. The third form is

```
onintr <label>
```

which causes any interrupt of the script to perform a jump to the "label:" statement, where execution in the script will resume.

The **nohup** command makes the script ignore "hangups" or attempts to "logout" of the session. Scripts that use this command continue to execute even if you end the session.

If jobs are running or waiting to run, and an attempt is made to end the session by logging out, a warning message will appear: "There are stopped jobs". If you ignore the message and attempt to log out again, the user session will terminate and the jobs will be removed. Jobs that are executing in the background are not affected by ending the user session unless they are waiting for input from the terminal. In that case, they too, will end. So if you want to execute some commands but don't want to wait for them to finish, you can run them in the background and logout without affecting their execution.

CONTROLLING THE PRIORITIES OF YOUR JOBS

The **nice** command can be used to adjust the job priority. If it is important for one job to finish before another, or for one job to run faster than another, the priority of the faster job can be raised.

The command

```
nice <command>
```

sets the priority of this job higher than the default priority. This causes the command to run faster than other jobs that are executing at the default priority.

## 11

Controlling the Flow Through Scripts

OVERVIEW

The C shell provides a number of C-like flow control facilities such as **foreach** loops and **while** loops to help perform repeated operations in a command script. The **foreach** loops process lists of items, and **while** loops will repeatedly execute a set of statements as long as a condition is true. Both controls can combine with **if** statements where appropriate to provide conditional control. This chapter examines looping structures.

In addition, this chapter covers the following commands:

- **break**
- **continue**
- **end**
- **exit**
- **foreach**
- **goto**
- **repeat**
- **while**

PROCESSING A LIST OF ITEMS (FOREACH LOOPS)

If you want to perform an operation on a list of items, the **foreach** command is appropriate. To illustrate the use of the

foreach loop structure, suppose it is desirable to list the files in our various directories and save the output in a file. Originally, either we specified each directory whose file we wanted to list, or we changed the working directory to the directory of interest. However, a command can be used to develop the list of directories, and the **foreach** command can then operate on each directory in turn. The command script would be based on a command structure that looks like

```
foreach object ("list of objects")
  -
  -
end
```

This indicates we want to perform some operations on a "list of objects". The operations to be performed are contained between the **foreach** and **end** commands. Every item in the list can be referred to by the name of the variable used in the **foreach** statement as the first argument after the command itself. In the following example, items in the list are referred to by the variable *object*. If their size is desired, the appropriate command is

```
foreach object ("list of files")
  ls -s $object
end
```

This refers to the variable *object* just as any variable is referred to. The list of items to operate on is specified in the second argument on the **foreach** command line, and is enclosed in parentheses. The **foreach** command ends with an **end** command, which must stand alone in the command script.

Any method of developing a list is acceptable. The use of "*" normally specifies all items in the directory. If it is essential to operate on a different directory and select just files ending in *.c*, create a **foreach** command like

```
foreach file (~/subdir/*.c)
```

This creates a list of the files in the ~/*subdir* directory that end in ".c". The list of items to process could be produced by executing a command. This is accomplished using the "'" operand. In this example,

```
foreach file ('grep tty /etc/inittab')
```

the list of items will be the output from the command **grep tty /etc/inittab**. The "'" indicates that what follows is a command to run, and that its output is to be used as input for the next operation. This is a quick way of pipelining commands. This function leads to the following script to print all source files in a particular directory.

```
foreach sourcefile ('ls ¬/subdir/*.c')
  prettyprint $sourcefile
end
```

Here, **prettyprint** is any program that nicely formats a source file. As the shell variable *sourcefile* is successively set to each item in the list, it can be modified or added to by any variable operation defined for the shell. The extension on the filename can be modified, for example.

To analyze the various directories in our directories, the following command script can be used.

```
#! /bin/csh -f
# Look through all of the entries in our current
# working directory. For any of the entries that are
# directories, we will change to that directory
# and analyze it.
foreach entry (*)
  # Make sure this is a directory.
  # The following test is described in chapter 14
  if (-d $entry) then
    # Change current working directory
    pushd $entry >& /dev/null
    # Tell what we are going to do
    echo "- - - - - - - - - - - - - - - - - - - - - -

    echo "- - Contents of $cwd directory follows - -"
    # Now list files with attributes
```

```
    ls -l
    # Now return to original directory
    popd >& /dev/null
  # End the if statement
  endif
# End the foreach command
end
```

Note that the **pushd** and **popd** commands are used to change to one particular directory, then return to the original directory. This is good practice in any command script. The current working directory will then be the same both before and after execution of the script. Unfortunately, both **pushd** and **popd** will write out the directory stack contents each time they are invoked. Thus, output from these commands is written to the */dev/null* file to make it disappear. Then that output will not be interspersed with the output we are really interested in. This is discussed in more detail in Chapter 13 when handling input and output in a command script is discussed.

   The items you want to operate on can also simply be listed in parentheses. In the following example, the attributes of files "file1", "file2", and "stuff1" are displayed.

```
    foreach f (file1 file2 stuff1)
      ls - l $f
    end
```

The **break** command can be used to leave a **foreach** loop before the **end** statement that delimits the loop. Execution resumes after the end of the nearest enclosing **foreach.** Thus, the progress of the **foreach** loop can be tested and, when some pre-established condition occurs, a decision can be made to exit it.

   Both the **foreach name (list)** command and the **end** command must stand alone on the line. It is also possible to nest **foreach** commands, and to combine them with **while** commands.

PERFORMING COMMANDS WHILE A CONDITION IS TRUE

The **while** loop checks on a condition and performs operations during that time the condition remains true. The **while** loop starts with

```
while (expression)
```

and ends with

```
end
```

just as the **foreach** loop ends.

The **while** loops are useful for performing an action over and over again until a particular condition is no longer true, or until some other condition occurs. The **while** loop will be performed until the expression contained in the **while** statement is false. The true/false test for a condition is performed every time the loop starts. Thus, the script

```
set number = 0
while ( $number < 5)
  # The following statement is described in chapter 14
  @ number + +
  echo "This is loop number $number"
  -
  - (Do your loop operations here)
  -
# End the while statement
end
```

can cause operations in the **while** loop to be executed five times, while the value of the variable *number* is less than or equal to five. Then the looping will end. The expression *number* + + increments the value of the variable *number* by one each time it is executed.

A **while** loop can be prematurely exited with the **break** command. Both the **while (expr)** and the **end** commands must be placed alone on a line.

EXITING FROM A WHILE OR FOREACH LOOP

The **break** command can be used to exit the **while** or **foreach** loop and resume execution after the nearest **end** statement. The **break** command is the usual one to employ to cause the premature end of a **while** or **foreach** loop. Thus, the previous example could be changed to

```
set number = 0
# Loop forever or until a forced exit occurs
  while ( 1 )
# Increment variable number by 1
  @ number + +
  echo "This is loop number $number"

  ˜(Do your loop operations here)

  # Test for doing loop again or not
  if (number >= 5) break
end
```

and the loop would stop after the fifth execution due to the execution of the **break** command. The use of **break** has an advantage: the condition that causes the **while** loop to stop can be complicated with several levels of **if** commands or other kinds of tests. Another way to use **break** is to search for some file and, when it is found, allow the loop to process it.

The **break** command will cause execution of a **while** or **foreach** loop to halt. Execution will resume after the **end** statement of the nearest enclosing **while** or **foreach** loop.

EXITING A COMMAND SCRIPT

Exit from a command script any time with the **exit** command. This command causes the command script to terminate no matter what type of loop you are in. You can also set the *status* shell variable so the command following the command script tests what the outcome of the command script was. Set the *status* shell variable with

```
exit (7)
```

which will set the *status* variable to seven. An expression can be enclosed in parentheses so as to exit with a variable value that depends, in some measure, on what was accomplished in the command script. For example, the statement

```
exit ( $value )
```

will end the command script with the *status* variable set to be the value of the *value* variable.

JUMPING TO A PARTICULAR STATEMENT IN A COMMAND SCRIPT

It is possible to transfer control to a particular statement during the execution of a command script. The transfer can also be forward or backward in a command script. Control will be transferred to the statement labeled label1 upon execution of

```
goto label1
```

Statements in a command script are thus labeled so control can be transferred to them with the **goto** command. The labeled statement is

```
label1: command arg1 arg2
```

The C shell interprets this as a line with a pointer to it. The *label* field can be indented with blanks or tabs for readability.

Tests with **if** statements, for example, are often combined to form conditional jumps. Thus

```
set laststatus = $status
if ( $laststatus == 0 ) goto good
```

```
if ( $laststatus = = 1 ) goto error1
if ($laststatus > 1 ) goto errors_all
```

provides a way to examine the returned status from a command and decide where to transfer to within the script to handle the error that was returned. Note that the first line of the example saves the status of the prior command for later processing. If the *status* variable is not saved at that point, processing the first **if** statement changes the value of the *status* variable and therefore needs to be captured before testing.

The label specified in the **goto** command will be filename and command name substituted before the execution of the **goto** command. Thus, the name of the statement to be executed next could be a variable containing the label to jump to. In the following example, where to jump to in the command script is determined by the value of the variable *choice*.

```
if < condition1 > set choice = statement1
if < condition2 > set choice = statement2
    -

   ˉ (Execute some commands)
    -

# Make sure variable is defined
# and if it is, transfer to a particular label
if ( $?choice ) goto $choice
    -

statement1:
  echo "At statement1"
    -

    -

statement2:
  echo "At statement2"
    -

    -
```

This approach is useful if the actual jump within the command script will not occur until later in the script.

CONTINUE STATEMENTS

When a **goto** statement is executed, the labelled line in the script that gets control might contain an executable command. It is possible though, that it is not necessary to perform any operation at that statement in the command script. For example, if you want to skip the execution of a few statements and jump to the end of a loop, use a **continue** command. The **continue** statement does nothing but continue the execution of the nearest enclosing **while** or **foreach** loop.

Thus, **continue** statements provide a method of directing a **goto** jump to a particular statement without actually executing commands when the jump takes place. This is a way of creating a labelled statement that executes no command.

REPEATING A COMMAND

Sometimes commands must be repeated. A **while** loop can be set up to do that, but a simpler method is to use the **repeat n** <**commandname**> statement where n is the number of times the commands that follow are to be repeated. For example,

```
repeat 10 echo ""
```

will cause the cursor on your terminal to move down ten blank lines. This type of command can format output to display on a terminal. Another way to use it is to signal the user about a problem. The command

```
repeat 10 echo "the TAPE is not loaded"
```

will display a warning message ten times on a user's terminal. This warning can be followed with a request that the user indicate when the "TAPE" is installed, and a message that execution of the script will be suspended until then.

USING FOREACH AND WHILE LOOPS
INTERACTIVELY

The two looping commands, **foreach** and **while**, can be used interactively. When entered, these commands will be responded to with a "?" prompt. Successive commands are then entered for execution during the loop. After a command is entered, another "?" prompt appears. If a blank line is entered by touching [RE-TURN], it gets stored and another "?" prompt appears. The end of the loop is caused by entering the **end** command in response to this "?" prompt, just as you would end a **foreach** or a **while** loop in a command script. Once the **end** statement is entered, the loop starts. The first pass through the loop tests the syntax of the various commands that have been entered. If you err while entering a statement but have not yet touched the [RETURN] key, you can rub out any characters in error. Once [RETURN] is touched, the statement is stored for later execution and can not be further modified. In addition, these statements are not entered in the history list. So if a set of statements is entered during a **while** loop and generates the output you are interested in, you can't save them for creating a command script later.

The initial command line containing the **foreach** and **while** commands is checked to be sure the syntax is correct, but no further processing occurs until the **end** statement is entered.

As an example, if you wish to copy all files in a directory whose names end in *src*, and, while you are doing that, you want to change the name of each file by starting each one with a "B", start your **foreach** loop with

```
foreach file ( *.src )
```

and the C shell responds with a "?" prompt. The following are the commands you enter successively.

```
echo "Copying the file: $file to new directory."
cp $file /usr/fred/save/B$file
end
```

After the **end** command is entered, the C shell will start the **foreach** loop and begin to copy the list of files to the new directory with a new name.

The **while** command operates the same way. Entering the command **while (1)** will cause the shell to reply with "?". Entering the following displays the time being used by any process that is running and attached to your terminal every ten seconds

```
ps
sleep 10
end
```

Since the expression specified for the **while** command will never be false, this command sequence runs until you interrupt it yourself. You will not be able to enter another command at your terminal until you halt this one, or interrupt it and put it in the background mode.

## 12

Testing Conditions
in Scripts

OVERVIEW

The C shell provides a number of C-like control facilities like **if** condition checking and **case** structures. These help control the flow through a command script. Alternate processing is often necessary, depending on file contents, to what values variables are set, or terminal response. All these types of control can combine with the **while** or **foreach** statements discussed in Chapter 11.

This chapter will cover the following commands:

- **breaksw**
- **case**
- **else**
- **endif**
- **endsw**
- **if**
- **switch**

TESTING CONDITIONS WITH THE IF COMMAND

Within command scripts, there is usually a need to test a condition and choose operations accordingly. The **if** command provides one way to perform this "test and choose" operation. The C shell provides three forms of the **if** statement. The simplest is

```
if ( expression ) command
```

where, when the expression is true, the one "command" that follows the expression will be executed, and when the expression is false, the "command" will not be executed. The "command" that can be given here can not include pipeline commands, can not be a list of commands, and can not be a parenthesized command list. Variables can be used in the "command" and substitution for them will take place upon testing the expression. One way to use this form of the **if** statement is to set a variable if it is not yet defined. The following command will test whether the variable *var1* is defined and set it to "define?itnow" if it is not:

```
if ( ! $?var1 ) set var1 = define?itnow
```

This form is useful for setting up variables and doing simple operations.

The second form of the **if** statement allows the specification of a number of commands to be performed when a condition is true. The following commands illustrate the syntax of this form:

```
if ( expression ) then
  command1
  command2
  command3
    ˉ (and so on)
endif
```

and the **endif** command marks the end of this **if** statement. Commands in this form of the **if** statement can be any structure including pipeline commands, command lists, etc. As an example, if you wanted to test whether a variable was set, and if it

was not, to set another variable and to issue a message, issue
the following commands

```
if ( ! $?varl ) then
  set varl = define?itnow
  echo "The variable 'varl' is now set to:   $varl"
endif
```

Executing this set of commands will ensure that the *var1* variable is **set** and that the user is notified when that value changed.
In addition, this form of **if** command can include **while** loops or
foreach loops.

The third form of the **if** statement allows one set of actions
to be taken if the expression tests true and another set of actions
if the expression tests false. The form of this **if** command adds
the **else** command to the previous form to provide alternative
commands. Thus, if it is desirable to print one message if the
variable was already defined, and a different one if it was not
already defined, use the following commands

```
if ( ! $?varl ) then
  set varl = defineditnow
  echo "The variable 'varl' is now\
                           set to: $varl"
else
  echo "The variable 'varl' was already\
                           set to: $varl"
endif
```

If the expression *! $?var1* is true, all of the statements to the
first **else** statement are executed and execution resumes after
the **endif** statement. If the expression is false, the execution of
commands starts after the **else** statement.

The **if-then-else** form of the **if** statement is useful for testing variables and making sure that they are set or combining
various **if** statements together to determine how to set a variable.
For example, the following will test the variable, and **set** it if it
is not set, and if it is **set**, will test how it is set and correct its
current value if it is not "defineditearlier":

```
#
#  Check to see if variable is not defined
#  If not, set it and tell user
if ( ! $?varl ) then
  set varl = defineditnow
  echo "The variable 'varl' is now set\ to: $varl"

#
# Now check to see if the variable
# was set to a particular value
#
else if ($varl == "defineditearlier" ) then
    echo "The variable 'varl' was already\
                          set to: $varl"

  else
    #
    # Finally do something else
    # if variable was not "defineditearlier"
    #
    set varl = makeitanewdefinition
    echo "The variable 'varl' was not\set to"
    echo "'defineditearlier' and is now\set to: $varl"
endif
```

Only one **endif** command is necessary. As many **else** and **else if** statements as you wish can be included and they are delimited by one **endif** command.

USING SWITCH STATEMENT TO CREATE CASE TESTING

Another type of testing can be performed which uses the **switch** command. The format is

```
switch ( string )

case strl:
   commandl
   command2
breaksw
```

```
case str2:
   command3
   command4
breaksw

• • •

default:
• • •
endsw
```

where **switch** defines the beginning of this structure and **endsw** defines the end of this structure. The *string* in the **switch** command is command and filename expanded. Then each of the various **case** commands are executed where the value of *string* is compared against the value of *str1, str2*, etc., until a match is found. When a match is found, the commands in that **case** are executed until the **breaksw** command is found. Then execution of commands resumes after the **endsw** command. If no matching **case** is found, then the **default** case is executed. If no **default** case is specified, then execution will continue after **endsw** command. This type of structure is analogous to the "case" structure used in C programs.

The "switch" type of command structure is most useful for executing a different sets of commands depending on the value of a variable which has been defined before executing this structure. For example, if you have a number of host computers to which you connect, you might want to define different variables depending on the system you are attached to. In the following command sequence, the **hostname** command output is tested to determine the name of your current host, and to perform some tasks while logged into that particular host. In this example, the main library of user–defined executables is in different directories, depending on the host. Thus, the *path* shell variable must be adjusted to reflect that. The command sequence for that looks like

```
# This script looks up the name of the host
# and defines variables for each of
# the different hosts.
```

```
#
# The variable system needs to contain just
# the name of the host. The first form is
# for systems where no routing information
# is contained in the hostname.
# The second form is for cases where
# some routing information is included.
set system = 'hostname'
# set system = 'hostname : sed 's/\..*//' '

# Start the 'case' type of structure
switch ($system)

case host1:
# Include here any commands specific to host1
# This system has my mail facility
  set mail= (30 /usr/mail/myname)
  set local =/usr/ucb
  breaksw

case host2:
# Include here any commands specific to host2
  set local =/usr/local
  breaksw

case default:
# Include here any commands that you would do
# if the host is not one of the above
  set local =/usr/uts
endsw

# Now define path based on what was figured out
set path = ($local /usr/bin /bin /usr/support.)
```

Other commands can be added for various hosts if specific operations are to be done on each of them. The **hostname** command is expected to contain just the name of your current host. (This might not be true for all systems. Sometimes routing information is included in the host name. An alternate form of the **hostname** command is provided in the prior example but is commented out.)

Another use for this structure is to define terminal characteristics so commands like **vi** and **more** work properly. To do this, it is necessary to examine the output from the **tty** command that returns the "device" on which you are executing. Note that this example uses a metacharacter (in this case, "*") to compare the **switch** string with the various **case** strings. This type of script looks like

```
#
#
switch ('tty')

case /dev/ttyp*:
  # terminal type is a pseudo terminal
  # which is usually assigned if you
  # are logged in on this system via network
  setenv TERM xterm
  breaksw

case /dev/tty8:
case /dev/tty9:
  # terminal is some kind of hard wired terminal
  # set up terminal characteristics
  setenv TERM vt100
  breaksw

case default:
  # terminal type didn't match our tests
  # notify the user
  echo "output from tty command is not recognized"
  set out='tty'
  echo "it is: $out"
endsw
```

If the terminal type is not recognized, notify the user.

Another use for the **switch** command is to process the reply to a request for input from the terminal user. The following script asks the terminal user for input and then parses it.

```
while (1)
  echo -n "Do you want to proceed? (y/n):"
  switch ("$<")
  case "n":
    set replace = "n"
    break
  case "y":
    set replace = "y"
    break
  endsw
end
```

This script takes advantage of a **while** loop to ensure that if the requested input is not an "n" or a "y", it will be requested again.

13

Handling Input and Output in Command Scripts

OVERVIEW

Input and output generated within a command script can be handled with facilities that can be used interactively while running individual commands at a terminal. Other facilities also exist, mainly for use in a command script. In particular, facilities are available to use output from the execution of commands as input for other commands. This chapter covers those subjects in addition to ways to handle input from a terminal while in a command script, and a way to make output from a command disappear.

REDIRECTING OUTPUT FROM A COMMAND SCRIPT

As discussed in Chapter 4, the ">" and ">>" operands can redirect output from a command or a command script. Because the ">" operand creates a new file (or empties an old one), use it if you want to save the output in a new file. However, if a number of commands are running, each of which will create output for one common file, use the ">" operand to create the file, then the ">>" operand to append further output to it. In the following script the first redirect operation (">") is the creation of the file. All others (">>") simply append other sets of output to the already created file before it goes to the printer.

```
#   ! /bin/csh -f
#   command file to print a document with a
#   common header and trailer on each file
#   Only argument to this script is name
#   of file to print

#   Define a file to put output into
#   Use \$\$ to create unique file name
set FC=/tmp/$$CC

#   First access of output file creates
#   a new file
cat start > $FC

# Further output into file is appended
cat $1 >> $FC

# Append trailer information
cat end >> $FC

# Now print the file you just created
lp -dlineprinter $FC

# Now erase the temporary file you created
rm $FC
```

The $$ shell variable is used in the sample script to ensure that the file being created will be unique to this process. Each invocation of this script will have a different process id. Thus, several copies of this command can run simultaneously, and each will create a uniquely named file.

To redirect diagnostic output or output that indicates what errors are occurring, add an "&" to the redirection operators (">" or ">>") to form ">&" and ">>&" operators. Since the previous script does not have the "&" included, all diagnostic output will be displayed on the terminal. This output can be saved into a file by redirecting it from the execution of this script into a file.

For example, if the script above is called **printit** and the document you want to print is called *doc33*, execute

```
printit doc33 >& doc33.errors &
```

which stores into file *doc33.errors* any output generated during the execution of command **printit doc33**. Since the standard output from script commands is being redirected into a file, the output that is not redirected will be diagnostic. The "&" at the end of the command executes it in background mode.

The shell variable *noclobber* controls whether or not a pre-existing file will be overwritten by operations performed within the command script.

MAKING UNWANTED OUTPUT DISAPPEAR

Some commands produce output that may not be very useful. Further, such output may interfere with the output you want. Fortunately, you can make it disappear by sending it to the infamous "bit bucket". In most systems, the */dev/null* file can be used as a "bit bucket" because any output written to it disappears. It is set up so any user can write to it.

In a command script you redirect unwanted output to the */dev/null* file. Two of the most troublesome commands are **pushd** and **popd**. Each time one of them is invoked, it outputs the current contents of the directory stack. In a command script this output is not useful. Yet you need these commands when you want to change to another directory. The script will want to return you to the original directory before exiting so script users will not be in a different directory after executing this command script. Output that tells the user what directory changes are taking place are not just undesirable, they are confusing. To solve this problem, redirect the output of each to the */dev/null* file to make it disappear. For example,

```
pushd newdir >& /dev/null
```

will change the directory silently by writing the output of the **pushd** command to the "bit bucket." You can execute script commands and return to the original directory afterward by including

```
popd >& /dev/null
```

which returns to the original directory silently. If you want to suppress the standard messages but still see diagnostic ones if any occur, leave out the "&" operator.

Another use of the */dev/null* file is to empty an existing file or create an empty one with

```
cp /dev/null /usr/fred/emptyfile
```

This empties the file */usr/fred/emptyfile* if it exists, or creates the file */usr/fred/emptyfile* if it does not.

REDIRECTING INPUT FROM THE TERMINAL

Sometimes it is useful to ask the command initiator for some input. This is a technique that can be used to build a script that will issue a set of commands depending on user response. But for this kind of command to work, the command initiator must be asked for some input.

To request input from the terminal, use the $< operator. That reads input from the keyboard. For example, if a reply from the user is desired before deleting a file, use the following command sequence:

```
while (1)
  echo -n "Do you want to proceed? (y/n):"
  switch ( "$<" )
  case "n":
    set replace = "n"
    break
  case "y":
    set replace = "y"
    break
  endsw
```

```
end
if ($replace = = "y") then rm <filename>
```

This command will continue to cycle, requesting a response from the user, until user input is a "y" or an "n". (The form of **echo** with the "-n" option is reviewed later in this chapter.)

BUILDING A FILE FROM INPUT LISTED IN A COMMAND SCRIPT

Sometimes it is convenient to create a file in a command script from input listed in the command script itself. To do this, redirect standard input into a command such as **cat** using the "<<" operator. After this operator, enter a string that will be searched for and signal the end of the input. Following the command itself, list the input in the order in which you expect the command to read it. For example, suppose you want to create a file of names in a command script. The command script will look like

```
cat > /tmp/stuff << EOF
sleepy
snoopy
droopy
clyde
EOF
```

and the file */tmp/stuff* will contain

```
sleepy
snoopy
droopy
clyde
```

but not the string "EOF". The "EOF" string simply signals the end of input into the **cat** command. Strings that will be input are variable substituted for, just as any variable is. Thus, if the value of the variable *name1* was "harry," the following command script

```
cat > /tmp/stuff1 << EOF
sleepy
$name1
droopy
clyde
EOF
```

creates the file */tmp/stuff1* that contains

```
sleepy
harry
droopy
clyde
```

but not "EOF" or $name1.

As another example, the stream editor **sed** will read commands from standard input to operate on a file whose changed output is then written to standard output. This can be a convenient way to edit a file that is output from another command. The command script looks like

```
#! /bin/csh
# The argument to this script is the name
# of the file to edit
sed $1 << EOF
s/a/b/
w
q
EOF
```

and will invoke the **sed** command to edit the file *filename* to change the first occurrence of "a" to "b" in each line, then write it out.

GENERATING OUTPUT TO DISPLAY ON A TERMINAL

The usual way to generate messages for display on a terminal is to use the **echo** command as it has been used in earlier chapters, like

```
% echo This will be displayed on a terminal
This will be displayed on a terminal

%
```

Variables can be inserted in the words to be echoed and will be substituted for. Often, the phrase to be shown is enclosed in double quotes ("). Earlier examples used substitution for variables as a way to show current variable values. For example

```
echo The value of the variable 'var1' is: $var1
```

displays the value of the variable *var1* at the end of the message.

An alternate form of the **echo** command adds an option "-n", which suppresses the newline at the end of the message so the cursor will be left at the end of the output line. This form of the **echo** command is useful for putting a message out on the terminal, and then asking the terminal user for a reply with the cursor placed at the end of the question.

It is good practice to display current values of the important variables while executing a command script. This can be done with a sequence of **echo** commands with substitution for the variables included in the messages.

If you need to write out control characters, the **/bin/echo** command is better equipped to write out sequences of characters the C shell **echo** command will be unable to.

If you want to write out some of the characters that have special meaning to the C shell, such as "$" or "(", you will have to "protect" them from interpretation as C shell operands. That is done by putting a "\" operator in front of them. Try

```
% echo This is a \$ sign \( Not a variable \).
This is a $ sign ( Not a variable ).

%
```

This includes the display of both the "$" and the "(" characters that the C shell uses for special purposes.

MANAGING READ/WRITE PERMISSION ON FILES CREATED

When files are created they have read/write permissions assigned to them. The *umask* shell variable controls the read/write permission on any file created by the command script. This "mask" field consists of three numbers. The first number controls read/write access to the file for the owner, the second controls read/write access for users in the same group as the owner, and the third controls read/write access for all others. Set the number to zero to grant everyone access to the file, to two to restrict write access, and to four to restrict read access. The typical *umask* field is *022*. That restricts write access to the owner.

USING OUTPUT OF ONE COMMAND AS INPUT TO ANOTHER

As discussed in Chapter 4, the pipe operator (|) connects the output of one command to the input of another. This facility can be used in command scripts as well. In addition, the operator " ' " (command substitution) can generate output from a command and use it for input to another command, or as an option to another command. For example, the following command will find out where a particular executable is stored, and then display its attributes.

```
ls -l 'which init'
```

It will do so without creating a temporary file or even a temporary variable. Of course, the output from other commands can be used to define shell variables. For example,

```
set printer_cmd = 'grep lpd /etc/inittab'
```

will look up one entry in a file with the command **grep** and will save that output as a shell variable.

USE OF EVAL AND EXEC COMMANDS

A command generated by executing another command can be executed within a command script with the **eval** command. For example, the output of the **resize** command (if your system has one) is a sequence of characters that reset the terminal variable. It is necessary to execute the sequence of characters after they are generated by the **resize** command. To accomplish this, issue

```
eval 'resize'
```

which executes whatever the **resize** command outputs. A command created by stringing together shell variables can also be executed with the **eval** command.

Another command can be executed in place of the current shell with the **exec** command.

## 14

Defining Your Own Expressions

OVERVIEW

As discussed in earlier chapters, expressions are used in various ways, especially as part of constructing **if** and **while** commands. For commands like **if** and **while**, conditions that must be tested are constructed as expressions. Usually these tests involve comparing variables to other variables or constants. A special set of tests can be constructed to check the attributes of files and directories. This chapter describes how to construct expressions to test conditions. In addition, it shows how to perform calculations by forming expressions and setting variables to the results.

DEFINING LOGICAL STRING COMPARISON EXPRESSIONS

To compare two character strings, the operands " $==$ ", " $!=$ ", " $=$ ̃", and "!̃" are available. Variables are defined as strings unless a calculation defines them. The proper type of comparison must be done, though. If the variable is a string, string operators must be used. An expression comparing two strings will look like

```
$fred = = "hello"
```

and will test to see if the variable *fred* is exactly equal to the string "hello". The logically opposite test is

```
$fred ! = "hello"
```

which tests to determine if the variable *fred* is not equal to the string "hello".

Another type of string comparison is one that tests to see if a variable matches a pattern with the metacharacters *, ?, or instances of [. . .]. Thus

```
$fred =~ "hel*"
```

will be true if the value of the variable *fred* started with "hel" and contained any number of letters. If you want to see if the variable *fred* contained the string "hel", use

```
$fred =~ "*hel*"
```

A more detailed discussion on how to use metacharacters to match patterns is found in Chapter 9. The "!~" operator tests whether or not the variable contains the "hel" string.

DEFINING NUMERIC COMPARISON EXPRESSIONS

To compare two numerical values, the operands ">" (greater than, "<" (less than), "= =" (equal), "<=" (less than or equal), and ">=" (greater than or equal) are provided by the C shell. For example,

```
$i > 5
```

tests whether the variable *i* is greater than five or not. If it is, this test returns one. If it is not, this test returns zero. Variables that have been set to the null string are considered equal to zero.

Only the first value of a multivalued variable is used in the comparison. All others are ignored.

TESTING WHETHER A VARIABLE IS DEFINED

One of the most useful expressions is one that tells you whether a variable is defined or not. Variables can be used as switches to control the flow through command scripts. To do that, it is necessary to define them with a certain value and then test whether they have that value later in the command script. However, if the variable is not defined, the command fails with the message "Variable not found." This is not particularly helpful to the user who invoked the command. It is much better to test whether the variable is defined and, if it is not, issue an informative message.

Variables can be used for communications between invocations of the C shell. So when you run a command script you may want to give it information for use during its operation. One way to do this is to put information on the command line. But that has its limits, and can be cumbersome if the number of arguments is large, or if the arguments are complicated. Another method of communicating between C shell invocations is to define environment variables before invoking the command script, test for them in the script, and use that information within the script itself.

To test whether a particular variable is defined or not, test the following expression.

```
$?varl
```

The sense of this expression can be reversed by adding the "!" logical operator. Thus

```
! $?varl
```

will be true when the variable is not defined, and false when it is. Here the "!" character is the "not" logical operator. The use of "!" to make the comparison opposite to what's expected must be followed by a blank, tab character, newline or "/". Otherwise, it will be taken as a "history" operator.

TESTING FILENAME ATTRIBUTES

The names of files or directories can be tested for particular attributes with tests of the "-t" form. Tests of this type are particularly useful when processing a list of filenames. These tests are usually used as expressions in **if** statements, such as

```
if ( -f $filename ) echo $filename is a file
```

which test whether the current value of the variable *filename* contains the name of a file. If the expression in parentheses is true, a message will be displayed indicating that the variable *filename* contains the name of a file. If the test is true, the value of the expression is "1" and the message will appear. If the test is false, the value of the expression is "0" and the clause following the **if** statement will not execute. The sense of the test can be reversed with the "!" (not) operator.

A number of different file attribute tests can be performed by changing the letter that follows the "-" in the example above. In that example you can test whether or not a variable contains an object name that is a file with the "-f" test. If you are examining the contents of a directory and want to know what are and aren't files, perform

```
if ( -f $filename )
```

This is only true when the variable *filename* contains the name of a "plain file" and not the name of a directory.

Test whether the name of an object is a directory with the "-d" test. Thus

```
if ( -d $filename ) echo $filename is a directory
```

prints a message if the variable *filename* is a directory and not a file. This type of test is useful if a particular directory is expected to exist. If it doesn't, you will create it.

You can test whether the object is an executable file by using the "-x" test on it. This test is useful if you are building a command script to create the name of a command from variables and want to make sure the command name you developed is executable so the script will not fail. If you try to execute a command that is not executable, you will receive the message "command not executable." For example

```
if ( -x /usr/bin/command1 ) /usr/bin/command1
```

will only execute **/usr/bin/command1** if that file is marked as executable. You can control which commands will execute in a script by controlling the executability of the various command files. Thus, to execute one command but not another, and to control which command will execute without changing the script, your command script should contain

```
if ( -x /usr/bin/command1 ) then
  /usr/bin/command1
  chmod -x /usr/bin/command2
else if ( -x /usr/bin/command2 ) /usr/bin/command2
endif
```

Using these commands, the executability of the two commands will be manipulated to execute only one. If you examine the system file */etc/rc*, you find that a number of command sequences are executed or not, based on whether a particular file is executable or not. Naturally, the choice of which commands to execute can be based instead on the value of some variables.

You can test whether a file exists or not by using the "-e" test. This is a useful way to see whether or not you are overwriting an existing file. It is also useful to ensure that if you need to read some input from a file it exists before you attempt to read from it. Obviously if it does not exist and you do not test for it, your script will fail and you will not be able to display a message indicating the problem. For example,

```
if ( ! -e file1 ) then
  echo The file $file1 does not exist and should
```

```
   exit (3)
endif
```

tests for the existence of a file. If it does not exist, the command script displays a message and exits with *status* shell variable set to three.

In addition to these tests, you can also test some other interesting file attributes. You can test whether you have read access to a file with the "-r" test, or whether you have write access to a file with the "-w" test. These tests help ensure that you will not try to read from a file you are not permitted access to, or write to a similar file. You can test whether a file contains nothing (if it exists) with the "-z" test. This is a good way to see if you should execute a file. First, define an empty file. Then, if conditions are right, fill it with a command script. Later, test for anything in the file. If there is, execute it. Finally, determine if you own it with the "-o" test. In all of these cases, if the file does not exist, the test will return false.

COMBINING EXPRESSIONS

Expressions to create tests with multiple conditions can be combined. The "&&" operator (logical "and") between two expressions requires both to be true before the whole test is true. For example, the command **do—it—now** in the statement

```
if ( $#argv = = 2 && $?TESTING ) do_it_now
```

will be executed only if both expressions are true. A third condition can be required by adding the "&&" operand and another expression.

The " | | " operator (logical "or") between two expressions requires only that one of the two expressions be true for the whole test to be true. Thus, the command **do—it—now** in the statement

```
if ( $#argv = = 2 | | $?TESTING ) do_it_now
```

will be executed if either expression is true. Again, a third condition can be involved by adding the " | | " operand and another expression.

The operands "&&" and " | | " can be combined for more complicated expressions. You should use parentheses to ensure that the correct set of conditions is tested for. In

```
if (( $#argv == 2 | | $?TESTING ) && -x do_it_now ) do_it_now
```

the command **do_it_now** will be executed only if one of the first two expressions and the third expression is true. If the parentheses around the first two expressions is omitted, a different set of true conditions is required for the command to be executed.

DEFINING NUMERICAL CALCULATIONS

Calculations can be performed during command scripts by creating expressions with operators such as $+$, $-$, $*$, $\backslash$, etcetera, and setting a variable to the result. The calculation is requested by using the character "@" as the operator. Thus,

```
@ var3 = ( $var1 * 4 ) / ( $var2 + 4 )
```

will perform a calculation to create a value for the variable *var3*. Use parentheses to ensure that the calculations are performed in the desired order. The numerical operators available in the C shell are " + " (addition), " − " (subtraction), "*" (multiplication), and "/" (division). For example, the following script will change kilobytes to bytes.

```
#! /bin/csh -f
# Only argument to script is number of kilobytes
#
@ bytes = $1 * 1024
#
echo $1 kilobytes is $bytes bytes
```

In addition, the "modulo" function can be applied with the "%" character as in

```
#! /bin/csh −f
set count = 0
while ( $count < 11 )
  @ count + +
  @ mod = $count % 7
  echo $count is $mod modulo 7.
end
```

which prints out the numbers 1 through 10, performing the "modulo 7" operation on each.

One special type of numerical expression can be used to increment and decrement variable values. These operators are "+ +" and "− −", and are similar to operators the c programming language provides. Thus

```
@ j + +
```

increments the variable *j*, and

```
@ j − −
```

decrements the variable *j*. Comparison can be made on the resultant value. The following loop would be executed five times.

```
set i = 0
while ( $i < 5 )
  @ i + +
  echo $i
end
```

Note that the expression "i < 5" is a numerical operator and compares the value of the variable *i* with the number 5. Each execution of the while loop will increment the value of the variable *i*.

15

Starting and Ending
User Sessions
Revisited

OVERVIEW

As discussed in Chapter 1, users are often presented with an *enter login*: prompt. Entering a user id with a password begins the user session. This chapter discusses in more detail what happens when a user session begins, what files to define to set up a user–specific environment of commands and C shell options, and what happens when a user session ends.

STARTING A USER SESSION REVISITED

When a user starts a session, after the name and password have been validated, a program that reads input from and writes output to the terminal starts. This program is usually a shell program. To start a session, an entry in a file called */etc/passwd* must be created. The user name and the password that validates the user is in this file. A particular initial command to be run for the user is specified, too. Typically the C shell is the program invoked (specifically **/bin/csh**). Once the C shell starts, a file called *.cshrc* is read and executed if it exists. This file must be in the user's "home" directory, which is also defined in the password file. Then, if this is a **login** operation, the *.login* file is read (again from the user's home directory) and executed, and finally the interactive prompt is displayed. Samples of both the *.cshrc* and *.login* files are discussed in Chapter 17.

Commands that set up a user environment can be stored in either the *.cshrc* file or the *.login* file since both are executed when a user session starts. However, since only the *.cshrc* file is executed when a command script is executed, those commands useful in a command script environment should go in the *.cshrc* file. For example, the definition of the *path* shell variable (where to find executables) is useful in the command script environment, whereas the definition of the terminal prompt is not. Extra commands in the *.cshrc* file will slow down command script initiation and should be avoided.

WHAT SHOULD THE *.CSHRC* FILE DO?

The *.cshrc* file is read and executed every time a new C shell starts. So any command scripts created to run under the C shell will be able to inherit any shell variables that have been defined if those variables were defined in the *.cshrc* file. Any shell variables defined by the user at the terminal *during a user session* will not be known to any subsequent C shell. However, environment variables defined in a user session *will* be known to any C shell that is started by a C shell that defined that environment variable.

You can define variables that contain strings for which you want to use shorthand notation. If there is a directory you refer to often with a long name, it's useful to have a way to refer to it that requires less typing. Such shorthand references are defined with the **setenv** command. These definitions are best located in the *.cshrc* file so they are available to C shell scripts you run. For example, if you depend on having a list of variables to refer to, you would use **setenv** commands to define them.

```
setenv M /usr/lib/macros
setenv L /usr/lib
```

But you should not put any commands that generate output here. If you want to show a list of **alias**ed commands on your terminal when you log in, you should put the **alias** command, which displays all currently defined aliases, in the *.login* file. If you want to show a list of variables that are defined in the *.cshrc* file, you would also put those commands in the *.login* file, because the *.cshrc* file is executed before the *.login* file is read.

Since objects defined by **set** commands are locally defined, they are unavailable to any subsequent C shell invocation. What this means in practical terms is that if you need to regularly become someone else via an **su** ("switch user") command, the only way the user you have become can inherit 'your' environment is to put those **set** commands in the *.cshrc* file. That file will be executed when a new C shell is started for the new user you have become. Unfortunately, the *root* user does not usually run under the C shell and this method causes *root* to inherit your environment.

Some internal C shell options are best defined in the *.cshrc* file, which is the place for the command

```
set noclobber
```

so files will not accidentally be overwritten with the ">" operand.

Another section in the *.cshrc* should be the definition of the **path** shell variable that gives you access to the executables in your system. This list of directories should include all directories with executables except the */etc* directory. The set of directories that will be searched to find an executable is best placed in this file. This is the *path* directory. If that definition was placed instead in the *.login* file, no other commands executed under a new C shell would have the path defined for them. Remember, every time you run a C shell command script, the *.cshrc* file is read and executed. The *cdpath* shell variable definition lists directories to be searched for the name of the subdirectory that is specified when the **cd** command is executed. Clearly, the subdirectory names in a particular directory should be unique compared to the names of the subdirectories in other listed directories. If the cdpath definition is placed in the *.cshrc* file, changing directories using this facility will be available within command scripts.

WHAT DOES THE *.LOGIN* FILE DO?

The *.login* file in the user's home directory is read and executed every time the **login** command is executed by the user.

Some of the internal C shell options are best defined in the *.cshrc* file. Thus, that is the place for

```
set notify
```

so any changes in the status of background jobs will be reported, for

```
set ignoreeof
```

so entering [CTRL] + D characters will not log you off, and the place for

```
set history = 100
```

so the last 100 commands will be remembered.

One section in the *.login* file defines the *TERM* variable used by a number of programs to find out the number and length of the lines in your terminal (or terminal window). To support some window systems, the actual size of the window can be calculated by the **resize** program. The result is used to set up the *TERM* variable. In some systems the **tset** command is used to set terminal characteristics up properly. In all these cases, these variables are important only for a terminal–oriented C shell—one that is executing a **login** command. Thus, these definitions belong in the *.login* file.

A number of variables are defined or not depending on which host you are logged into. These variables are placed in appropriate parts of a **switch** command that has different sections for each host. For example, one networked news facility is read by the **rn** command with the *RNINIT* variable to define some of its parameters. The definition of this variable should be in the *.login* file, to be executed on the host you read that news on. As another example, the definition of the *mail* shell variable is usually in the *.login* file, to be executed on the host you read mail on.

The **pushd** command can be used to create a stack of directories to switch to with one command. This stack of directories is particularly useful in an interactive terminal–oriented session started by *.login*. Thus, setting up this directory stack is done in the *.login* command.

Since the *.login* file is read in and executed every time a new user session starts, it is the perfect place to store all commands that define any special commands or to redefine any built-in commands. As discussed in Chapter 6, the **alias** command can define or redefine any command. The *.login* file is the place for all **alias**es you have created. These aliases would look like

```
alias lf 'ls -aF'
alias pu 'pushd \!* ; lf; cd .'
alias po 'popd \!* ; lf; cd .'
alias pushd 'pushd \!*; cd .'
alias popd 'popd \!*; cd .'
```

and would define a set of aliases and a set of variables.

The next item for the *.login* file is the reading in of an old history file. Those lines in the *.login* file look like

```
if ( -e .hist.saved) then
  source -h .hist.saved
endif
```

which check first to make sure there is a file of history commands to read in, and then uses the **source** command to read them in, but not to execute them. If the user expects to use several hosts, it is desirable to save and restore different history files.

Another section in the *.login* file will be the display of the variables and aliases that have been defined. To do this, the following commands would display two variables defined in the *.cshrc* file, and all aliases currently defined.

```
# Now for any variables that might be of interest
echo "The following variables are defined:"
echo "M = $M"
echo "L = $L"
echo "The following aliases are defined:"
alias
date
```

The time and date would be displayed with the **date** command.

The definition of the prompt that is seen at the terminal also needs to be added. At the very least, the prompt must contain the name of the current host being and the number of the history command being run. Thus, the minimum definition of the terminal prompt would be

```
set hn = 'hostname'
set prompt = "${hn}: %"
```

which defines a variable to contain the host name and uses that variable with the "%" sign to display the current history command number. The variable *hn* may need to be defined differently if the **hostname** command on a particular system returns an answer more complicated than just the name of the host. The output generated by the **hostname** command can be edited like

```
set hn = 'hostname : sed -e 's/\..*//'
```

which removes other network information if it is present.

SETTING A "PATH" FOR FINDING EXECUTABLES

As described earlier, the list of directories to search for a particular executable or command script is defined with the *path* shell variable. Usually this variable is defined in the *.cshrc* file. When the *path* variable is set in the *.cshrc* file, a hash table is created. That table contains the names of the executables found in the various directories to provide rapid access to them. If any commands are added to these directories, the C shell will not know about them. It will be necessary to use the **rehash** command to inform the C shell that a new table of executables must be constructed.

The use of this table of executables can be disabled by issuing the **unhash** command. When that is done, the name of every command that is executed will have to be fully qualified. The same function can be accomplished in a command script with the "-f" option when the C shell for a particular command is started.

How well the table of executables is working can be discovered with the **hashstat** command. That command displays statistics where executables have been found.

SETTING UP A SEARCH PATH FOR A SUBDIRECTORY

The C shell can be given a list of directories to examine when the subdirectory specified is not in the current working directory. If the subdirectory you want to change to does not exist in the current directory, the shell will examine each directory specified in the *cdpath* variable to see if any one contains a subdirectory *source*. If the subdirectory does not exist in any of those directories, you will receive the "No such directory" message.

Thus, the variable *cdpath* can be set to a list of directories for investigation when searching for a particular subdirectory. This search feature is particularly useful if you tend to name your subdirectories uniquely. For example, if the only subdirectory *doc* you are interested in is in the directory */usr/lib/macros*, that directory should be one that is defined in the *cdpath* variable. If the following command was entered,

```
set cdpath = (/usr/lib/macros /usr/include /usr/spool)
```

to set up the search path for subdirectories, then entering the command **cd doc** sets your current working directory to */usr/lib/macros/doc*. If *lp* was a subdirectory of */usr/spool*, entering **cd lp** will change your current working directory to */usr/spool/lp*.

Using **cd** commands, the C shell will not remember any of the directories you were in previously. To return to a directory you were working in previously, you must use the **cd** command again, specifying the directory you want.

READING IN A FILE OF COMMANDS WITHOUT EXECUTING THEM

When a file of commands is read in, they are usually executed. However, when starting a session, it is desirable to establish a history of commands that have been executed. A file of commands can be read in without executing them with the **source -h** command. This is the complement of the **history -h** command, which saves the history file at the end of a session by issuing the **logout** command.

The **source -h** command reads in a file of commands but does not execute them. Instead, it places them on the "history" list as if they had been executed. This way, a new user session with a detailed history of prior commands can be started. If this is not done, the history file will be empty when the session is starts.

ENDING A USER SESSION REVISITED

When a user session is ended with the **logout** command, the *.logout* file is read and executed. Thus, it is the place for any needed activities when you end a session. The principal activity is to save the "history" file so it can be restored later.

## 16

Displaying and Managing Resource Usage

OVERVIEW

The use of system resources, such as cpu time and input/output operations, can not only be analyzed, but controlled. This chapter reviews the facilities the C shell provides to display what system resources are being used and how they can be managed.

This chapter will cover the following commands:

- **hashstat**
- **limit**
- **time**
- **unlimit**

DISPLAYING RESOURCE USAGE

The resources used during the execution of a C shell command can be displayed in one of three ways; by executing the command **time** after the command is finished, by executing the command under the **time** command itself, as in

```
time <commandname>
```

and by setting the shell variable *time*. Executing the command **time** after the command is finished and executing the command under the shell command **time** both produce a resource summary for that command only. But once the shell variable *time* is **set**, every command you execute will be followed by a one line summary of what resources that command has consumed.

The summary of system resources used will be displayed as

```
1.2u 11.7s 1:11 5% 41+23k 55+30io 19pf+0w
```

The contents of this one line display are

```
Field #1: user cpu time, in seconds
Field #2: system cpu time, in seconds
Field #3: elapsed time, in minutes:seconds
Field #4: ratio of cpu time/elapsed time
Field #5: memory usage for text area
                        and data area, in kilobytes
Field #6: input and output activity, in blocks
Field #7: page faults and swap outs
```

Thus, you can determine if the command you executed was input/output bound versus cpu bound; how much cpu time versus elapsed time was used; how many input/output operations were caused; etcetera. If you plan to develop a command to use over and over again, it is important to know what resources it uses.

In addition, you can use the *time* shell variable for reports on cpu time usage by setting the variable to the number of seconds after which you wish to be notified of the command's resource usage. Thus

```
set time=5
```

ensures that any command that consumes more than five cpu seconds produces the one line resource usage summary. If you do not give a value when you **set** the variable *time*, the resource of every command will be displayed.

CHANGING THE DISPLAY
OF SYSTEM RESOURCE USAGE

The standard display of resources used by a command may not include all you want to know—you may not be interested in "swap or page" operations, for instance. You can tailor the display by setting display characteristics when you **set** the shell variable *time*. The normal format of the command that will not change the display of system resources is

```
set time = n
```

where n is the number of seconds of cpu time that triggers a display. This form of **set**ting the **time** variable will offer the display

```
%Uu %Ss %E %P %X + %Dk %I + %Oio %Fpf + %Ww
```

The way to change the display is with

```
set time = (5 "%Uu %Ss %I + %O")
```

where *%Uu %Ss %I + %O* describes what you want the display to look like. The possible choices for this display are

```
%U   user cpu time
%S   system cpu time
%E   elapsed time
%P   percentage utilization (cpu time/elapsed time)
%X   text size/cpu seconds
%D   data size/cpu seconds
%K   image size/cpu size
%M   maximum image size
%I   number of input blocks
%O   number of output blocks
%F   number of hard page faults
%R   number of page reclaims
%W   number of swap-outs
```

Each of these can be followed by units of measure or be combined. If you merely want to see elapsed, user, and system cpu times, and input and output counts if the command used more than 3 cpu seconds, issue

```
set time = (3 "%E %Us %Ss %Ii + %Oo")
```

Then, once a command has lasted over three cpu seconds, you would see

```
03:04 3.5s 0.5s 345i + 53o
```

indicating that this command took three minutes and four seconds to run, used 3.5 user cpu seconds and 0.5 system cpu seconds, and performed 345 input and 53 output operations.

LIMITING RESOURCE USAGE

Limitations on resource usage can be set up with the shell command **limit**. The format for the command to limit usage of cpu time is

```
limit cputime 5
```

which limits the cputime available to that shell and any process it creates to five cpu seconds. The type of resources and the name used to limit them is

cputime	maximum number of cpu seconds
filesize	size of largest file created
datasize	maximum size of data+stack region beyond text size
stacksize	maximum size of stack region
coredumpsize	maximum size of a core dump
memoryuse	maximum size of working set size

Any of these names can be shortened to a unique string and placed in the **limit** command. For any resources that can be limited, the units of measure are kilobytes, except for "cputime" which is expressed in seconds. The current limitation on any of these categories can be displayed by issuing

```
limit <resourcename>
```

Issuing the **limit** command without any resource name will display all resources and their current limiting values.

Core dumps are generated by programs when their execution fails due to one of a number of possible errors. Generally, these files are not too useful unless you are debugging a C program. One use of the *coredumpsize* resource is to disable the creation of core dumps by setting the limitation on this resource to zero (0). Then no core dump files can be created. This is desirable for many users.

Limitations on a particular resource can be lifted by issuing

```
unlimit <resourcename>
```

Issuing the **unlimit** command by itself removes all restrictions on resource usage.

DETERMINING THE EFFICIENCY OF THE PATH DIRECTORY LIST

On some systems a C shell command **hashstat** will display statistics on how efficient the list of directories you have specified for finding executables (the *path* shell variable) is in locating commands you execute. The output from this command is

```
12 hits, 14 misses, 46%
```

which indicates that in requesting commands to execute (commands not built into the C shell), the chance of finding the executable in the list of directories specified by the *path* variable was 46%. This means that, on average, every time an executable was requested at least one directory in addition to the correct one was searched.

It is possible that the directories at the front of the list do not contain many executables you use, but later directories do. Changing the order of the list may increase the percentage of times an earlier directory contains the executable of interest.

## 17

Example Command Scripts

OVERVIEW

Sample command scripts are better ways of illustrating the principles of doing a particular job than by describing how to get that job done. This chapter illustrates the principles of designing good command scripts by listing some well designed examples. First a sample *.cshrc* file and a sample *.login* file will be shown. Then an assortment of other command scripts are listed.

EXAMPLE .CSHRC FILE

The following is a sample *.cshrc* file that illustrates how a *.cshrc* file should be constructed. Comments have been added to further explain some of its contents.

```
#    The following definition is to show that
#    the .login file is executed after the
#    .cshrc file
set checkit = "cshrc does it"

#    This definition of the name of the host may
```

```
#   need to be adjusted to match the way your
#   host names are defined.
set SYSTEM='hostname'

#   What follows is a testing of the host into
#   which we are logged so that the path to
#   executables can be matched to the system
#   into which you are logged
#
#   Also will set up a variable path to
#   subdirectories via cdpath

switch ( $SYSTEM )
#   Notice that two case tests can have the
#   same code executed
case host1:
case host2:
   setenv BIN /u/fred/programs/bin
   setenv SRC /usr/lib/src
   setenv UBIN /u/local
   setenv DIR /u/local/source
   breaksw
case host3:
   setenv BIN    /u/harry/programs/bin
   setenv SRC    /usr/support/src
   setenv UBIN   /u/local/bin
   setenv DIR    /usr/local/source
   breaksw
#   Need to define these so that the path
#   declaration will work on all hosts default:
   setenv BIN    /u/root/programs/bin
   setenv SRC    /usr/lib/src
   setenv UBIN   /u/local
   setenv DIR    /usr/local/source
endsw
#   Now that we know where the executables are _
#   we will set up path to them
set path=( . /usr/local $UBIN   /bin  /usr/  bin /usr/ucb $SRC \
   $BIN ~/bin )
```

```
#
#    Now we define the path for subdirectories
#    Some of these are fairly common directories
#
set cdpath = ( /usr/include /usr/spool $DIR\
    /usr/lib/macros )
#
#    Make sure that files are not overwritten
#    accidentally
set noclobber
```

Other commands can be in the *.cshrc* file in addition to those listed above. Experiment with what's in your *.cshrc* until you are comfortable with it.

SAMPLE .LOGIN FILE

The following is an example of how to construct a *.login* file. As in the sample *.cshrc* file above, a number of the commands in this one are executed only on a particular host. Since an interactive session is initiated with a **login** command, the *.login* file is the place to set up the terminal characteristics, and to display some of the aliases and environment variables defined for this session.

```
#    To show .login is executed
#    after .cshrc
set checkit="login does it"

#    Now define some of the shell variables
#    of interest
#
#    Make sure that changes in our jobs
#    are reported immediately
set notify
#    Set the size of the history file to
#    something reasonable
set history = 100
```

```
#    Make sure that [CTRL]+D will not end
#    the user session
set ignoreeof

#    Set the terminal characteristics
switch ('tty')
case /dev/ttyp* :
   tset -s -Q >/tmp/tset$$
   source /tmp/tset$$
   rm /tmp/tset$$
   breaksw
endsw
#    If there is a window system setup DISPLAY
#    variable
if ($TERM == "xterm" ) then
  if (! $?DISPLAY) setenv DISPLAY $SYSTEM:0.0
  set noglob
  eval 'resize'
  unset noglob
endif
#
#    set up a number which is for history
#    file save/restore
set termtty = 'tty'
set termnumber = $termtty:t
#
#    Check for system and adjust any
#    environment variables that are
#    special for this system
switch ( $SYSTEM )
case host1:
  setenv myname $USER
  #    read in history file
  #    follow convention in .logout file
  #    for name of history file
  if ( -e hist.A.$termnumber) then
    source -h hist.A.$termnumber
  endif
  breaksw
```

```
case host2:
  setenv myname $LOGNAME
  #   read in history file
  #   follow convention in .logout file
  #   for name of history file
  if ( -e hist.B.$termnumber) then
    source -h hist.B.$termnumber
  endif
  breaksw

case host3:
  #
  #   This is system that receives mail
  #   for this user so make sure we get
  #   notified; check every 5 minutes
set mail = ( 5 /usr/mail/$LOGNAME)
  setenv myname $LOGNAME
  #
  #   This is the host to read news at
  #   so set up rn ENVIRONMENT variables
  #
  setenv RNINIT "-e -m -N -S"
  setenv SAVEDIR "%p/%C"
  setenv SAVENAME "%a"
  #
  #   read in history file
  if ( -e hist.C.$termnumber) then
    source -h hist.C.$termnumber
  endif
  #
  #   Set up a stack of directories
  #   Add directories to this list as you
  #   use them
  #
  pushd ~/newrel >& /dev/null
  pushd ~/newrel/ftp >& /dev/null
  pushd ~/newrel/bin/all >& /dev/null
  pushd ~/oldrel/bins >& /dev/null
  #   Make sure you set the directory back
```

```
#    to home directory
pushd ˜ >& /dev/null
#    Now print out the directory stack
echo "The current directory stack is:"
dirs
breaksw

default:
  setenv myname $LOGNAME
endsw
#
#   Define some ALIASES
#
#   Add some commands which are set up
#   the way you want them
alias lf 'ls -aF'
alias h20 'history 20'

#    Add a command with the defaults that you
#    would like for "pg"
alias mpg 'pg -s -p "Page %d [Hit RETURN]" \!*'

set hn = 'hostname'
#   Now set up your terminal prompt to
#   show which user, which host, and
#   the lowest two levels of the
#   current working directory
#   (The following should be one line)
alias cd 'cd \!* ; set cwdh = $cwd:h ;
  set prompt = "$hn [$cwdh:t/$cwd:t/] \! # "'

cd .
alias pu 'pushd \!* ; lf; cd .'
alias po 'popd \!* ; lf; cd .'
alias pushd 'pushd \!*; cd .'
alias popd 'popd \!*; cd .'
#
# Print all aliases to remind you
#
echo " _ "
echo "The following ALIASES are set:"
```

```
echo " "
echo "Alias Meaning "
alias
```

Thus, the *.login* file sets up the directory stack, displays it, defines aliases and displays them, and sets the terminal environment.

SAMPLE .LOGOUT FILE

The *.logout* file is executed every time a user ends a terminal session with the **logout** command. It is, then, the place to save the current "history" of commands. What follows is an example of how a *.logout* file should be constructed.

```
#
# Save your history file by system name
# when you end a user session
#
# This script depends on the fact that
# two variables were already defined:
#
# SYSTEM: the name of the host
# termnumber: the end of the device name
#
switch ( $SYSTEM )
case host1:
  history -h > ~/hist.A.$termnumber
  breaksw
case host2:
  history -h > ~/hist.B.$termnumber
  breaksw
case host3:
  history -h > ~/hist.C.$termnumber
  breaksw
default:

endsw
```

This script will save the current history file into a file that is based on both the name of the host, and the name of the device you are executing on. This way, if you need to move to different devices on the same system, you can retrieve the same history file. These saved history files are then restored in the *.login* file when the user session starts.

SAMPLE SCRIPT TO DISPLAY DIRECTORY HIERARCHY

This script displays the hierarchy of directories that has been created below a selected directory. This particular script needs an **awk** program to space out the directory names shown after the C shell script.

Some sample output from this combination of a C shell script and an awk program looks like

```
Analyzing directories within /usr/fred
Mail
  files
Samples
  programs
      save
      current
  sources
bin
memos
  oldstuff
  newstuff
programs
xstuff
```

Note that the directories are sorted before display.

The C shell script is

```
#! /bin/csh -f
#    This script is adapted from something
#    that appeared in Unix world, 6/89, p 131
#
```

```
#    USAGE = "Usage: $0 [directory]"
#
if ( $#argv < 1 ) then
  echo No directory specified.
  echo Execution aborted.
  #    If you include special characters
  #    in output, you will have to protect
  #    them from the C shell.
  echo Usage: dirtree \<directory\>
  exit 1
endif
#    Move to directory to show hierarchy
pushd $1 >& /dev/null
#
#    save current dir
#
if ( -d $1 ) then
    set cdir = 'pwd'
else
  echo $1 is not a directory
  exit 1
endif

#
#    Set up temporary file to save output in
echo " Analyzing directories within $1 "> /tmp/$$DD
#
#    Locate all directories, sort names, save
#    in a temporary file to pass
#    to awk program to print nicely
#    formatted report
#
find . -type d -print | sort >> /tmp/$$DD

#
#    Format output using an awk script
#    to space directory listing in a nice indented
#    format
#
awk -f ~/dirtree.awk /tmp/$$DD
```

```
#    Return to original directory
popd >& /dev/null
#    Remove temporary file
rm /tmp/$$DD
```

The **find** command will list and process file names in a variety of ways. The command is used here to "print" all the names of the subdirectories in a directory with the "-type d" option.

The **awk** program referred to by *dirtree.awk* in the previous example is

```
BEGIN { FS = "/" }
NR = = 1 { IFS = "/" ; print $0; next}
NF = = 1 { next }
NR > 1 {
{
for (count = 1; count < NF; count + + )
  printf "";
}
print $NF
}
```

This sample **awk** program examines the names of the directories passed to it, and searches for the directory name at the lowest level of the hierarchy. As it parses the name at each level, it prints out five spaces. When it reaches the lowest level, the program prints out the name of the directory. The output is thus indented for every level it moves down.

SAMPLE SCRIPT TO DECOMPOSE A FILE NAME

This sample script illustrates a number of ideas discussed earlier. Its overall goal is to decompose the full path name of any file into all its various components, then to reconstruct the full path name in a different format. It does nothing useful with the decomposed file name; substitute your own ideas . . .

```
#! /bin/csh −f
#    Check out the contents of a directory
```

```
#    Break apart filenames into their parts

#    Argument on command line is
#    directory to examine

#    First step is to check for the expected
#    command line argument and print a message
#    indicating what is expected.
#
if ( $#argv < 1 ) then
  echo No directory is specified
  echo Usage: $0 \<dirname\>
  echo Execution is aborted
  exit 1
endif
#
#    Save the directory to search
set dir = $argv[1]
#
#    Make sure this is really a directory
#    If this is not a directory, give an
#    error which is different
#
if ( ! -d $dir ) then
  echo $dir is not a directory
  echo Usage: $0 \<dirname\>
  echo Execution is aborted
  exit 2
endif
#
#    Make sure user knows what you are
#    doing
echo ────────────────────────────────────────
echo    Checking the directory: $dir
echo ────────────────────────────────────────
#
#    Look at every file in the directory named
#
foreach file ( ${dir}/* )
#    (For convenience the foreach loop is not
```

```
#    indented.)
#
#    Unset any variables that we might have
#    used in previous loops that we may not
#    be setting every time through this loop
#
unset *tail
#
#    Skip any directories in this directory
#
if ( ! -d $file ) then
  echo ————————————————————————
  echo    Checking FILENAME = $file
  echo ————————————————————————
  set tail=$file:t
  echo The file name without path name /
    is $tail
  set ext=$file:e
  echo The file extension is $ext
  set head=$file:h
  echo The full path name without file /
    name is $head
  set ptail=$head:t
  echo The lowest level directory is /
    $ptail
  set headhead=$head:h
  echo The full path name without lowest /
    level directory is $headhead
  set pptail=$headhead:t
  echo The second lowest level directory /
    is $pptail
  set headheadhead=$headhead:h
  #    Check to determine if we have removed
  #    enough directories levels from
  #    name of file and if not get
  #    another directory level
  if ($headheadhead != $headhead ) then
    set ppptail=$headheadhead:t
```

```
        echo The third lowest level / directory is
        $ppptail
endif
set root = $file:r
echo The file name without extension /
  \(if there is one\) is $root
set tailroot = $root:t
echo The name of file without path /
  and extension is $tailroot
echo ─────────────────────────────────
          echo -n Now reconstruct file name /
  with "::" instead of "/" and
echo  ".." instead of "."
if ( $?ppptail ) then
  if ( $ext == "" ) then echo " ${ppptail}::${pptail}::
      /${ptail}||${tailroot}"
    else
      echo " ${ppptail}||${pptail}|| /
          ${ptail}||${tailroot}..${ext}"
    endif
  else
    echo " ${pptail}||${ptail}|| /${tailroot}..${ext}"
    endif
    echo ─────────────────────────────
  else
    echo $file is a directory
  endif
end
```

A sampling of output from this command looks like

```
- - - - - - - - - - - - - - - - - - - - - - - - - - - - -
═══════════════════════════════════════════════════════════
Checking the directory: ufred
═══════════════════ - - - - - - - - - - - - - -
─────────────────────────────────────
ufredMail is a directory
ufredNews is a directory
ufredaix is a directory
═══════════════════════════════════════════════════════════
```

```
Checking FILENAME = ufredcnfgrep1.ps
The file name without path name
     is cnfgrep1.ps
The file extension is ps
The full path name without file name
     is ufred
The lowest level directory is fred
The full path name without lowest level
     directory is u
The second lowest level directory is u
The third lowest level directory is
The file name without extension (if there is
     one) is ufredcnfgrep1
The name of file without path and extension
     is cnfgrep1

Now reconstruct file name with :: instead of and..
     instead
     of .
::u::fred::cnfgrep1..ps
```

This is the output for one file. Every other file will produce the same kind of output.

Test this kind of command by running it against several directories. Adjust the output commands until you see output that is exactly what you want.

SAMPLE SCRIPT TO GET INPUT FROM TERMINAL

In Chapter 13, an example is given that describes how to ask for input from a terminal user and how to parse that answer. That example is more profusely illustrated here with **while** and **switch** commands.

```
#! /bin/csh -f
#
#   This is a script which asks for input
#   and parses it and then will exit with an
#   appropriate status.
```

```
#
while (-1)
  echo -n "Do you want to exit with status 0? (y/n):"
  switch ( "$<" )
    case "n":
      echo A nonzero Exit is requested.
      set exitreq = "n"
      break
    case "y":
      echo Exit 0 is requested.
      set exitreq = "y"
      break
    default:
      echo Answer was not understood; try again.
  endsw
end
if ( $exitreq == "n" ) then
    exit (1)
else exit 0
endif
```

18

C Shell Messages

OVERVIEW

The C shell exists to perform the commands you have requested, but sometimes problems occur due to errors in the commands, errors in the syntax of the commands, or errors that other parts of the system recognize. The C shell has a collection of messages it can produce that notify you of problems it has recognized. These messages are written to "standard error" and thus can be managed as users redirect them to a terminal or a file. Such messages should remain separate from messages that are expected and are normally written to "standard out."

DETAILED DESCRIPTION OF C SHELL MESSAGES

An alphabetical summary of the most common C shell messages, with their meanings explained, follows.

<$ line too long: Input from the terminal is too long to be managed by the C shell.

<< terminator not found: Redirected input to a command was

not terminated properly. Error is probably due to failure of the C shell to find the expected termination field in the input stream.

 # hits, # misses, #%: This is an output message from the **hashstat** command (see Chapter 16) summarizing the efficiency of the current definition of the *path* shell variable.

Already stopped: An attempt has been made to issue a **stop** command to a job that has been stopped already. This is usually preceded by the number of the job.

Alias loop: An attempt to define an **alias** that will cause a loop in the definition of aliases has been detected.

Arg list too long: An argument list developed for a **foreach** command from another command is too long to be processed. Normally the limit for argument list length is 1024 bytes.

Arguments should be jobs or process id's: Argument for a **kill** command must be either the process id of a command, or the number the C shell assigns. Use the **jobs** command to determine the job number. Use some form of the **ps** command to determine the process id of the command to be signalled.

Argument too large, Arguments too long: The length of the argument(s) to a **while** or **foreach** command exceed the size of the storage buffer. This buffer is usually 1024 bytes long.

Bad signal number: An attempt to use the **kill** command to send a signal to a job or process has failed because the signal number was not valid. Use **kill −1** to see a list of valid signals.

Bad ! arg selector: The characters that follow the "!nnn:" field in your reference to a prior command are either not a number, or are a number that is greater than the number of arguments in that command.

Bad ! form: An error has occurred in the specification of the letters following the "!" in an attempt to refer to a prior command in the history file.

Bad ! modifier:: A modifier that is not valid has been specified, following the reference to a particular command. The valid modifiers are *e, g, h, p, q, r, s, t, x, &,* or a number equal to or less than the number of arguments in the command line.

Broken pipe: Pipe operation is incomplete due to some pipeline processes unexpectedly terminating. The message may also appear if a pipeline process is halted with a **kill** command prematurely.

Can't << within ()'s: An attempt has been made to redirect input in an implied subshell (one enclosed in parentheses) that can not be performed by the C shell.

Command not found: An attempt has been made to execute a command that cannot be found in any directory specified by the *path* shell variable.

Cputime limit exceeded: The cputime limit set by the **limit** command has been exceeded.

Directory not empty: A directory can not be removed if it is not empty, and an attempt has been made to delete such a directory. "Hidden" files (ones that begin with a ".") may still exist in the directory. Use **ls -a** to display hidden files.

Directory stack empty: An attempt has been made to perform the **popd** command to change a directory to one on the directory stack, but there are no directories on the stack.

Directory stack not that deep: An attempt has been made to change to a directory that is past the end of the directory stack. This error is usually due to executing the **popd +n** command with "n" greater than the number of directories on the stack. Use the **dirs** command to examine the stack and correct the command.

Empty if: No statements have been found in the **if** statement that has been parsed.

end not found: A **while** was not properly terminated with an **end** command. The **end** command must be alone on the line.

endsw not found: A **switch** command was not properly terminated with an **endsw** command.

Event not found: Reference has been made to a nonexistent previous command that was expected to be found in the *history* file.

<filename>: File exists: An attempt to create a new file has failed because the file already exists. This error may be due to the shell variable *noclobber* being set and an attempt made to redirect output to an already existing file.

File not found: The filename specified could not be located by the C shell.

File name too long: A file name you have specified or created by substitution exceeds its allowable internal maximum length. This length differs from system to system.

Filesize limit exceeded: The maximum file size specified by the **limit** command has been exceeded.

Interrupted: The execution of a job has been suspended by entering [CTRL] + Y characters, or by sending the INTR signal to a job executing in the background. The job can be restarted in the foreground with the **fg** command or in the background with the **bg** command. If no action is taken, the job will continue to be halted. If the user session is ended, the job will be terminated.

Is a directory: An attempt has been made to redirect output to a file that already exists as a directory.

Label not found: An attempt has been made to branch to a labelled statement that does not exist.

Missing): Parentheses used to delimit conditional phrases for an **if**, **while**, or **foreach** command need to be paired.

Missing file name: An attempt has been made to perform redirection but no file name was specified.

Missing name for redirect: A specification of the redirection of input or output from or into a file was not followed by the name of a file.

Modifier failed: An attempt has been made to use a history function to modify a previous command and reexecute it. Often the use of "ˆ" fails because the pattern to change does not exist in the prior command.

Mount device busy: An attempt has been made to unmount a filesystem but some file in it is open. The directory you are in is open and if your current directory is in that filesystem, the **umount** command will fail. This is an operating system message.

No current job: An attempt to refer to the current job with the command **bg** or **fg** will fail if there is no job currently interrupted.

No job matches pattern: An attempt has been made to refer to a job currently processing by the name of the command it is processing, but no command matches the specified pattern.

No match: An attempt to locate a file with a "globbing" operation found no file whose name matched the pattern specified. If the shell variable *nonomatch* is not set, this type of failure in a command script will halt the script.

Not enough core: An attempt to execute a process failed because no more swap space was available in the system. (This is actually an operating system message.)

Not login shell: An attempt has been made to end an **su** command by entering the **logout** command. While the execution of the **su** command starts another shell, it is not necessarily a "login" shell. Enter "exit" or the [CTRL] + D characters to end the **su** command.

Permission denied: An attempt to execute a command script that has not been marked executable will fail. Use the **chmod** command to mark the file executable.

Read-only file system: An attempt has been made to write to a file in a file system that is mounted "read-only." Use the **/etc/mount** command to examine how that system was mounted.

Stopped: A job has been interrupted and its processing halted with the [CTRL] + Y characters as it was executing in the foreground.

Stopped (signal): A job executing in the background has received the INTR signal via the **kill** command. The job will halt and wait for another signal, such as CONT (continue), to resume processing.

Stopped (tty input): A job executing in the background is waiting for input from the terminal. Such a job will not continue processing until it has been brought into the foreground and receives the input.

Stopped (tty output): A job running in the background wants to send output to the terminal but can't because it is executing in the background and the output was not redirected.

Subscript error: An attempt has been made to use an invalid value for a subscript, such as a negative or a character string value.

Subscript out of range: An attempt has been made to use a subscript for a multivalued variable larger than the number of variables it contains.

Syntax error: An attempt has been made to use the **foreach** command that is not properly formatted.

Terminated: A job has been executing in the background and has received the HALT signal.

Text file busy: An attempt has been made to create a new version of an executable file that is currently being executed. Usually this message occurs when linking a new version of a program still being executed. Halt the program execution and relink the program.

then/endif not found: An **if** command has been improperly terminated with a **then** phrase or an **endif** command.

There are stopped jobs: Jobs have been halted but not restarted. To see the jobs that have been "stopped," issue the **dirs** command. You can still end the session with the **logout** command. All "stopped" jobs will then be terminated.

Undefined variable: Reference has been made with the "$" notation to a variable that has not been previously defined.

Unknown signal; kill -1 lists signals: The first argument to the **kill** command was neither numeric nor one of a small group of four letter strings.

Use "exit" to leave csh.: An attempt has been made to end a C shell that is not a "login" C shell.

Use "logout" to logout: When the *ignoreeof* shell variable is set, entering the [CTRL] + D characters will not end a user session. Only entering the **logout** command will end it.

You have new mail: A file has been changed in the directory that is specified by the *mail* shell variable.

19

Tricks of the UNIX Trade

OVERVIEW

The basic idea of this chapter is to discuss some operations that are easy to do in UNIX but only if you know how to do them.

EXPANDING TABS SO A PRINTER WILL PRINT THE OUTPUT NICELY

Some printers ignore tab characters. That table that looked perfect on the terminal prints in little run-together pieces all gathered on the left side of the page. How can this problem be overcome?

The simplest way is to use a utility that turns tab characters into spaces. On some systems the utility **pr** will expand these tabs into blanks using the command

```
pr -e
```

So a pipeline like

```
cat file1 | pr -e | lp -dsomewhere
```

expands the tab characters into blanks on their way to being printed. Thus, the file will still display properly on a terminal, and will print nicely on a printer that disregards tabs. On some systems a slightly different program called **expand** accomplishes the same operation.

FINDING A STRING IN A FILE BUT ONLY REMEMBERING SOME OF THEM

Suppose you want to examine a file and find only some lines that contain a particular string of characters. Say you are developing a file of **set** commands that all your users will use, and you want to give examples of all types of **set** operations. In addition, you have provided comments describing each operation the same way the sample *.cshrc* file is organized (see Chapter 17). Operations that are not yet tested would be commented out with a "#". You want to list all **set** operations that are currently being done. Thus, you want to see all lines with the string "set" that do not contain "#".

The first thing you need to do is to pick out all lines in the file that contain the string of interest. This is usually done with a **grep** command as in

```
grep <string> <filename>
```

All lines in the file that contain the string of interest will be shown. Now you want to exclude those lines that contain a second string. You can accomplish that with

```
grep -v <anotherstring> <filename>
```

which uses the "v" option of the **grep** command to exclude lines that contain a certain string. Now combine them to get just those lines that contain one string but *not* the other. This pipeline command would be

```
grep <str1> <filename> | grep -v <str2>
```

which displays all lines that contain "str1" but do not contain "str2". To further illustrate the use of the **grep** command, suppose you want to halt the execution of all commands that start with "mytest" so you can recompile and link them. The following pipeline produces a list of those executing commands

```
ps -e | grep mytest
```

Unfortunately this list will include commands that contain the string "mytest" and will contain an entry for the command "grep mytest". A shorter list, generated by

```
ps -e | grep mytest | grep -v grep
```

will contain entries for only those commands that contain the phrase "mytest".

DISPLAYING ONE FIELD FROM A RECORD WITH MULTIPLE FIELDS

Often, output from various programs contains a number of fields in each record. Sometimes you are interested only in particular fields. What will retrieve only the fields we want?

One method is to use one of the capabilities of the **awk** command. This program is usually found as part of the UNIX tool set and has multiple capabilities. In fact, it could be the subject of another book. One function **awk** provides is the ability to treat each field in a record separately. For example, to print just the first field in a record where each field is separated from the others by blanks, execute

```
awk "{print $1}" <filename>
```

and just the first field in each record will be displayed. If you want the second field, change "$1" to "$2". If you want the second and the fifth, execute

```
awk "{print $2,$5}" <filename>
```

Earlier in this chapter, we constructed a pipeline that contains the names of commands we wanted to halt. If you want to halt the process with the **kill** command, you need to know the process id. If you pass the output of the **ps** command to the **kill** command, you have to select the field from the **ps** command that contains the process id. This is the first field. Thus, the full pipeline

```
ps -e | grep mytest | grep -v grep | awk "{print
$1}"
```

will produce a list that contains only process ids.

MARKING ALL OF THE DIFFERENCES IN A FILE

In preparing documents that must be reviewed several times, it is usual to show bars in the right margin ("change bars") when these documents are reissued. The bars indicate which lines in the document have changed since the previous version. Bars can be added as you make changes. However, that requires you to remember to mark all changes as you make them. When you are ready to send your document out again, you might not remember if you did mark them all. In addition, you might like to verify the changes you made.

One way to compare two files and get a list of the line–by–line differences between them is to use the familiar **diff** command. This produces a list of which lines are different and what changes to make to one file to produce the other. This output can be used to determine which lines changed. Then you can add the change bars yourself.

A better way to accomplish the same goal is to use the **diffmk** command. This compares two files and produces a third file that contains the contents of the first with change bars indicating which lines differ from the second.

The syntax of the **diffmk** command is

```
diffmk <newerfile> <olderfile> <markedfile>
```

The output of the **diffmk** command uses the **troff** command ".mc" to mark the various lines in the file. The **diffmk** command can mark with an "*" where lines were removed from the older file, and mark with a "+" where lines were added.

For an example, suppose the file you started with looked like

```
line 1
line 2
line 3
line 4
line 5
line 6
```

and you have edited it to look like

```
line 1
new line 2
line 3
line 4
line 4 A
line 5
```

Now you run

```
diffmk -a+ -c\ | newerfile olderfile markedfile
```

which compares the two files and marks with "+" those lines that have been added, and with ":" those lines that were modified. You end up with a file that looks like

```
line 1
.mc :
new line 2
.mc
line 3
line 4
.mc +
```

```
line 4 A
.mc
line 5
.mc *
.mc
```

When printed using troff command this indicates that "line 4 A" has been added while "new line 2" has been modified, and that something has been deleted after "line 5". The **diffmk** command operates literally. If you add punctuation or correct spelling or capitalization, **diffmk** will put in change bars to indicate the modification. Thus, **diffmk** usually errs on the side of pointing out differences that may or may not be there. You should "correct" the output of **diffmk** to properly reflect changes that have been made.

DISPLAYING THE KINDS OF FILES IN A DIRECTORY

One of the first commands you learned was probably the **ls** command. The list of options this command has is quite long. Buried in that list are two options that are among the most useful. One option indicates both whether a file is a directory or not, and whether a file is executable or not. This is the "F" option. It takes only one extra character to indicate those characteristics, so the directory listing will still be shown in five–column format. A second option ensures that every file in the directory is shown in the directory listing. The default for the **ls** command is not to show any file that starts with a ".". Thus, files like *.cshrc* and *.login* are called "hidden" files and are usually input for other programs in the system. The "a" option will show all files in a directory, even the ".." and "." files. In the *.cshrc* file that is given in Chapter 17 an alias for the **ls** command is defined. That alias sets the options for the **ls** command to be "aF" so all this valuable information is displayed.

As an example, the following is a listing of the directory using the **ls** command without any options.

```
Mail        backup       config      demo3.0A   letters
News        backup_demo30 cprogreams dialset    list_of_files
aix         bin          crash       ft.gantt   rel30
aliases     bugstuff     crash.list  jocko_login reports
aliases1    buster       crash.out   hist.C.ttyp0 route_command
aliases2    catlist      dead.letter hist.M.tty0 routes
ama         cngfrep1.ps  demo2.1     ipckill
awkscripts  cnfig        demo3.0     junk
```

The following is a listing of the same directory, but the command used in this case was **ls -aF**

```
./          .oldnewsrc ama/       cprograms/   host.C.ttyp0
../         .rnlast    awkscripts/ crash*       hist.m.tty0
.Newsrc     .rnsoft    backup      crash.list   ipckill
.Xdefaults  .rshrc     backup_demo30 crash.out  junk@
.alias      .twmrc     bin/        dead.letter  letters/
.db/        Mail/      bugstuff/   demo2.1/     list_of_files
.exrc       News/      buster/     demo3.0/     rel30
.letter     aix/       catlist     demo3.0A/    reports
.login      aliases    cnfgrep1.ps dialset*     route_command@
.logout*    aliases1   cnfig       ft.gantt     routes
.newsrc     aliases2   config      jocko_login
```

Note that this second listing has the same number of columns. Thus you get to see the same output, but the information it provides is much better. You will know that entries such as *Mail, News, aix,* etcetera are directories (indicated by a "/") and that entries such as *crash, dialset,* and *ipckill* are executables (indicated by a "*"). You will even know that "junk" is an entry that is not a file at all but a symbolic link to a file (indicated by a "@"). In addition, you will see that there are a number of other files in this directory you did not know you had, because the "a" option displays all directory entries that begin with ".". All this information comes at very little cost.

TRANSLATING LOWER CASE FILENAMES TO UPPER CASE

When you bring files from one operating system to another, the file naming conventions vary, and it is nice to be able to change the names so they look conventional. Most UNIX systems, for example, are case sensitive. That means that names that contain uppercase characters are distinct from names that contain the same characters in lower case. In some operating systems that is not so and all filenames are in upper case. If you copy files from such a system, filenames will be uppercase letters and numbers. The following is a way to modify your filenames to meet your needs. In this example, lower case file names change to upper case names.

```
#!/bin/csh -f
#
foreach i (*)
  mv $i 'echo $1 | tr a-z A-Z'
end
```

This script is another illustration of the output of one command being used as part of another. In this script the output of translating the name from lower to upper case is used as the new file name. Any other type of name conversion could be performed by simply replacing the **"tr"** command with some other command, such as **"sed"**.

EXECUTING SED COMMANDS IN A COMMAND SCRIPT

The **sed** command (sometimes called the "stream editor") can modify text files by replacing character strings with other character strings. Many commands **sed** provides can be used while editing a file with **vi**. However, if the output of a command script is not quite correct, and you want to edit it while still in the command script, you can execute **sed** and pass in the text manipulations you want. For example, say an earlier file contained

```
line 1
.mc |
new line 2
.mc
line 3
```

```
line 4
.mc +
line 4 A
.mc
line 5
.mc *
.mc
```

and you want to change all occurrences of "line" to "string" and all occurrences of "4" to "40." The following command would accomplish that.

```
sed -e 's/line/string/' -e 's/4/40/' input > output
```

Add to the command line every command you want **sed** to execute with the "-e" ("execute") option. Any number of these commands can be executed in the same execution as the **sed** command.

BECOMING ANOTHER USER (ROOT) FOR ONE COMMAND

Occasionally it is necessary to become "root" to change the attributes of some file. You can of course, enter

```
su root
```

and reply with the password to become "root". But usually you will only want to perform one command. If you first execute **su root**, then issue the command you want, you have to return to your former user name with the **exit** command. In addition, when you use this sequence of commands, the only command that appears in the history file will be the **su root** command you started with.

An alternate method is to use a form of the **su** command that lets you become another user for just one command. The proper syntax for this is

```
su root -c "chown system *"
```

This operation causes you to become "root," executes the command enclosed in ""s, and returns you to your prior identity. If your "root" user is password–protected, you will be asked to enter the password after you enter this command, just as if you had logged in as "root".

The full command string is recorded in the history file. Thus, if you need to rerun a particular command, it will be available via the usual history operations. However, all commands you execute as another user are recorded in a different history file, and are lost when you end that session.

PUTTING SPECIAL CHARACTERS INTO OUTPUT MESSAGES

The C shell built-in **echo** command does not easily enable you to put special characters, such as a tab or a newline character, or any ASCII character, into an output message (or into a file if it is redirected). However, the set of UNIX tools includes another **echo** command, one usually found in the **/bin** directory. This **echo** command lets you enter special characters with one of the following character sequences where the special character is wanted.

```
\c     print line without new-line
\f     replaced with form-feed character
\n     replaced with newline character
\t     replaced with tab character
\xxx   replaced with ASCII code which is the octal
       number xxx (which must start with a zero)
```

The replacement occurs when the output is generated. Thus, the following command would display output on two lines.

```
/bin/echo "This will be the first line.
               \nThis will be the second line"
```

Note that all input for the **echo** command is enclosed in double quotes.

Index